THE 4 DAY WEEK HANDBOOK

Joe Ryle

First published by Canbury Press 2024
This edition published 2024

Canbury Press
Kingston upon Thames, Surrey, United Kingdom
www.canburypress.com

Printed and bound in Great Britain
Typeset in Athelas (body), Futura PT (heading)

This is a work of non-fiction

FSC® helps take care of forests for future generations.

ISBN:
Paperback 9781914487194
Ebook 9781914487200

THE 4 DAY WEEK HANDBOOK

Your Guide to Happy Staff, Smarter Working and a Productivity Miracle

Joe Ryle

Contents

This book is dedicated to the late David Graeber, whose ideas and unwavering support hugely shaped today's movement for a shorter working week.

David Rolfe Graeber (1961–2020)

Introduction: What is the Four-Day Week and Where Does it Come From?

"For many ages to come the old Adam will be so strong in us that everybody will need to do some work if he is to be contented. We shall do more things for ourselves than is usual with the rich to-day, only too glad to have small duties and tasks and routines. But beyond this, we shall endeavour to spread the bread thin on the butter – to make what work there is still to be done to be as widely shared as possible. Three-hour shifts or a fifteen-hour week may put off the problem for a great while. For three hours a day is quite enough to satisfy the old Adam in most of us!"

John Maynard Keynes, *Economic Possibilities for our Grandchildren*, 1930

The aim of this book is to help you imagine or implement a four-day working week, with no loss of pay for workers, at the organisation you work for.

Chapters One and Two set out the case for a four-day week, highlighting existing evidence from trials that have taken place all over the world.

In Chapter Three we begin delving into the practicalities, looking at different models and approaches. Then we'll look at the type of challenges that can arise as we go through the process: preparing for a trial, finding ways to improve business performance to help enable the shift, before finally running a trial and then measuring its success. Then, before the conclusion, there's some information for employees interested in trying to organise for a four-day week in their workplace.

Whether you have only just started thinking about the four-day week, are interested but want to know more or are fully signed up to the idea already, this book is for you. For those of you raring to go, I hope it can guide you on your journey to a happier and more productive workforce. It is drawn from years of experience working with hundreds of four-day week organisations across the United Kingdom and evidence from around the world.

. . .

To better understand the growing momentum behind demands for a four-day working week, I want to begin by casting our minds into the past for some perspective on the way work has come to shape and dominate our lives today.

Foraging and making necklaces were the first human activities to be defined as work. The first foraging communities worked on average 15 hours a week, a far cry from today's working patterns which sees workers across the globe putting in anything from 40 hours per week to 100 hours per week (if you are unfortunate enough to find yourself working as a junior banker at Goldman Sachs.)[1] Despite all the progress of the last few centuries, how have we managed to get the balance so spectacularly wrong when it comes to working time?

Four key developments mark the progression of work throughout history: fire, agriculture, towns and cities, and heavy industry. This is not intended to be a history book so I will skim over the history quite quickly. When humans first mastered fire – around a million years ago, opportunities that never previously existed, to cook, stay warm and create light, arose. It also reduced the amount of time needed for hunting food, giving our ancestors more leisure time. This helped pave the way for the development of language and culture, including music and art.

Around 12,000 years ago, society reorganised itself around agriculture. This was an era of scarcity when people had to work hard in the fields to put food on the table. According to James Suzman, anthropologist and author of *Work: A History of How We Spend Our Time*, the shift to agriculture *"reveals how much of the formal economic architecture around which we organise our working lives today had its origins in*

[1.] https://www.theguardian.com/business/2021/aug/02/goldman-sachs-raises-pay-for-junior-bankers-after-100-hour-week-complaints

farming."[2] It also tells us a lot about *"how intimately our ideas around equality and status are bound into our attitudes to work."* Any of us who have met someone new recently will know this is accurate from the first thing we almost certainly asked them: 'what do you do?' – which really means 'what is your job?' I'll explain why this needs to change later in the chapter.

The next big reorientation of working life happened 8,000 years ago, when people began to gather in cities and towns. *"The birth of the first cities seeded the genesis of a whole new range of skills, professions, jobs and trades,"* James Suzman says. The final major reorientation was heavy industry – fossil fuels unlocked new material possibilities and factories and mills sprang up in cities, causing a surge in the size of their populations. As a result, we all became a lot busier – primarily through our work.

By the 19th century, workers across the world were putting in, on average, anything between 60 to 90 hours per week. In 1884, the Federation of Organized Trades and Labor Unions urged all American workers to observe an eight-hour day after a huge mobilisation campaign by anarchists, socialists and trade unionists. Their slogan, which was initially coined by Welsh textile manufacturer Robert Owen in 1817, was: "Eight hours labour, eight hours recreation, eight hours rest." Prior to this, a working day could range from anything between 10 to 16 hours for most people. Just over one hundred years ago, as society continued developing, most people worked six days a week – with Sunday reserved as the

---

[2] James Suzman, *Work: A History of How We Spend Our Time* (London: Bloomsbury, 2020)

day of prayer. In fact, the weekend only became a concept towards the end of the 19th century.

After a major campaign led by the trade union movement and some progressive businesses, the weekend was won for all workers between the 1920s and 1940s, depending on the industry you worked in and which country you called home. The cheering crowds that can be heard every Saturday afternoon as football matches kick off across the country were another major factor in the successful campaign to win the weekend. The weekly fixture cemented the idea Saturday was a day for leisure.

So the 9–5, five-day working week, otherwise known as the 40-hour week, was born. Many British people take the weekend we have today for granted, but it's important to remember that campaigners fought hard so we could enjoy our weekends.

The 40-hour week soon spread across Europe and the rest of the world. We know very little about how much international coordination took place and through which channels it was organised, but we do know that the United States of America and Spain led the way internationally.

Ford Motor Company

One of the first pioneers of the 40-hour week was the Ford Motor Company in the United States. On the 1st of May, 1926, Ford became the first major company in America to adopt a five-day, forty-hour week for workers in its automotive factories. Henry Ford, the founder of the company, took his six-days a week operation down to five, with no loss of pay for the workforce. He was hoping the change would result in greater productivity and that people would have more time for leisure activities such as shopping.

In a 1926 interview Henry Ford said: *"leisure is an indispensable ingredient in a growing consumer market because working people need to have enough free time to find uses for consumer products, including automobiles."* The funny thing about this quote is it cheekily suggests that he believed his employees would be more likely to spend their hard-earned cash on buying more of his cars if they had more spare time on their hands. He later said: *"it is high time to rid ourselves of the notion that leisure for workmen is either 'lost time' or a class privilege."*

Though workers' time at work was reduced, productivity went up and manufacturers all over the country soon followed Ford's lead. Edsel Ford, Henry's Ford's son and the company's president, said at the time:

"Every man needs more than one day a week for rest and recreation. We believe that in order to live properly,

every man should have more time to spend with his family."

In 1938, the Fair Labor Standards Act was enacted by Congress to reduce the work week to 40 hours.

. . .

Closer to home, John Boot, the Chairman of Boots cosmetics company, based in England, initiated the same experiment. Again, he found that two days off each week had a positive effect on productivity and reduced absenteeism. The weekend was made official Boots policy in 1934.

Those arguing against a 40-hour week at the time made arguments such as; 'the economy will suffer,' 'businesses won't be able to afford it' and 'workers won't be able to adapt.' The same arguments we hear today against a four-day working week. But these arguments were proved wrong then and hopefully by the time you get to the end of this book you will realise they are wrong again now.

It is important to remember that the 9–5, five-day working week was primarily designed for the agricultural and industrial economy we had at the time. No one can argue that the economy hasn't transformed since then, but for some reason – I have my suspicions – working hours have not transformed too.

Calls for a four-day working week are not new, but they have been given a new lease of life in the wake of the Covid pandemic. Most people won't know that one of the first national figures to call for a four-day work week was former

Republican President of the USA, Richard Nixon.[3] As Vice President in 1956, he said he foresaw a four-day work week in the *"not too distant future"* to create a fuller family life for every American. He said: *"These are not dreams or idle boasts, they are simple projections of the gains we have made in the last four years. Our hope is to double everyone's standard of living in ten years."*

What the Vice President is alluding to here is the relationship between economic productivity and leisure time; this basic logic has underpinned the economy for centuries. The theory goes that as the economy experiences greater productivity, workers should benefit from more leisure time because the productivity gains should reduce the amount of labour time needed. This was the premise by which famous mainstream economist John Maynard Keynes predicted in his essay, *Economic Possibilities for our Grandchildren*, that by 2030, we would all be working only 15 hours per week. A prediction, that, without some very dramatic changes occurring between now and 2030, is almost certainly going to be proven wildly inaccurate.

So what has happened? Despite all the productivity gains of the last century, why are we still working a similar amount of hours as we were 100 years ago?

The 9–5, five-day working week still remains the norm across most of the world. According to the Chartered Institute of Personnel and Development (CIPD), over 60 per cent of jobs in the UK still operate using this model.[4]

[3.] https://www.nytimes.com/1956/09/23/archives/nixon-foresees-4day-work-week-says-gop-policies-assure-fuller-life.html

[4.] https://www.cipd.org/uk/knowledge/reports/four-day-week/

Working hours drifted down from the 1930s to the beginning of the 1980s, but then it all started going wrong. Analysis by the New Economics Foundation (NEF) shows very clearly that average weekly hours fell a lot slower post-1980.[5] According to NEF, the UK would have been on target to reach a 30-hour week by 2040 had average hours continued to fall in line with the initial post-war trend.

During the three decades following World War Two, a combination of increased pay and productivity, strong collective bargaining and increased labour market regulation saw the average full-time week in the UK fall from 46 hours in 1946 to 40 hours by 1979. However, from 1980 onwards, this trend faltered following labour market deregulation, Margaret Thatcher's attacks on trade union rights and slower earnings growth for low income workers. As a result, by 2016 the average full-time week fell by just two and a half hours to an average of 37.5 hours.

What this effectively means is that most productivity gains since the 1980s have gone towards greater company profits, rather than more free time for workers. Let that sink in without trying not to get angry! When you take into account the additional labour added to the economy as a result of huge numbers of women joining the workforce, it's even more shocking. In the early 1970s, female employment was at 52.8 per cent but by the first quarter of 2023, it was

---

[5.] https://neweconomics.org/2019/03/average-weekly-hours-fell-faster-between-1946-and-1979-than-post-1980

72.3.[6] Despite all of those extra hours being put in, working hours haven't reduced accordingly.

In the UK, we now work some of the longest hours in the world.[7] We work longer full-time hours than any country in the European Union (excluding Greece and Austria)[8], while having one of the least productive economies. To make matters worse, we also have the fewest bank holidays. This would all be a lot easier to accept if living standards were rising but the opposite is happening – living standards are falling.

Research by Barclays Bank released in 2023 showed how British workers have missed out on a Europe-wide trend toward more leisure time and fewer hours at work. According to Barclays' analysis, on average, working hours in the UK have only fallen by five per cent over the past four decades. This means we're now working 27 per cent more hours on average than Germany. Over the same time period, working hours fell by 10 per cent in France, Italy and Spain.

All the evidence points to the fact that all these long working hours aren't producing good economic results. What they are producing, however, is a workforce where millions are burnt out, stressed, overworked and not to be too dramatic but – in some cases – dying. This is no way to live and no way to run an economy. Around 18 million

---

[6] https://www.statista.com/statistics/280120/employment-rate-in-the-uk-by-gender/#statisticContainer

[7] https://www.tuc.org.uk/news/british-workers-putting-longest-hours-eu-tuc-analysis-finds

[8] https://progressiveeconomyforum.com/wp-content/uploads/2019/08/PEF_Skidelsky_How_to_achieve_shorter_working_hours.pdf

working days are lost every year in the UK as a result of work-related stress, depression and anxiety, according to the Health and Safety Executive[1].

UK and US Workers Reduced Their Hours Least in Recent Decades

Annual working hours per worker, 1982=100

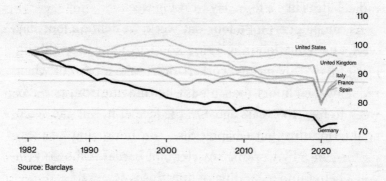

Source: Barclays

In 2021, the first global study of its kind showed that long working hours are killing hundreds of thousands of people around the world every year.[9] According to the World Health Organisation (WHO)[10], long working hours led to 745,000 deaths from stroke and heart disease in 2016, a 29 per cent increase since 2000. The study, conducted with the International Labour Organization (ILO), showed almost three-quarters of those who died were middle-aged or older men. Most of these deaths were in South East Asia and the Western Pacific but the data had implications for the UK as well.

[9.] https://www.bbc.co.uk/news/business-57139434

[10.] https://www.who.int/news/item/17-05-2021-long-working-hours-increasing-deaths-from-heart-disease-and-stroke-who-ilo#:~:text=Long%20working%20hours%20led%20to,published%20in%20Environment%20International%20today

For the first time in my lifetime, the Covid pandemic shone a spotlight on many of these issues. It goes without saying that the pandemic was an awful time for everyone but it undoubtedly generated sweeping changes to the world of work which were long overdue and may have never taken place without a pandemic. It also left the door open to more radical ideas like a four-day working week.

As campaigners for a four-day week, we define a four-day week as a reduction in working hours to 32 or less, with no loss of pay. This means workers don't take a pay cut when reducing their hours, the same as when moving from a six-day week to five, 100 years ago. On the face of it, this can seem counterintuitive but Chapter Six – on improving business performance by working smarter, not harder – should give you a better understanding of how this is achievable.

What happened in the workplace during Covid was nothing short of remarkable. Almost overnight, most of the population began working from home, a shift which would have been completely unimaginable before the pandemic. At the scheme's peak, 30 per cent of the workforce were having their wages directly paid by the Government[11] – otherwise known as Furlough.

Workers all across the country had their first taste of more freedom and autonomy at work, and it felt good. It's important to note that of course not everyone experienced this. Key workers and those that couldn't work from home went into work as normal. Others lost their jobs. But for

---

[11.] https://www.ons.gov.uk/employmentandlabourmarket/ peopleinwork/employmentandemployeetypes/articles/ anoverviewofworkerswhowerefurloughedintheuk/october2021

those that did see their working life dramatically changed overnight, it had a profound effect. Workers saw for perhaps the first time in their lives that when we want the world of work to change, it can happen very fast. What the move to remote working also showed is that workers can adjust to new ways of working fairly quickly and with relatively little pain. Many with long journeys to work got two hours or more back from no longer having to commute each day.

It was already the case before Covid that workers could request more flexible working and the popularity of this has certainly grown since the pandemic. The right to request flexible working was first introduced under the Flexible Working Regulations Act 2014, giving workers the legal right to request flexible working from their employer. This act has recently been updated to give workers the right to request flexible working from the very first day of employment. The organisation Pregnant Then Screwed and tireless campaigner Mother Pukka deserve much of the credit for that recent change in the law.

Under the existing guidance, types of flexible working include: job sharing, working from home, part-time, compressed hours, flexitime, annualised hours, staggered hours and phased retirement. We know that flexible working can benefit both employers and employees as it has been shown to increase job satisfaction and improve job recruitment.[12] However, I would argue that the currently accepted forms of flexible working do relatively little to improve productivity and mental wellbeing. Because what

---

[12.] https://www.acas.org.uk/new-study-reveals-half-of-employers-expect-more-flexible-working-after-pandemic

they don't do is get to the root cause of the main problem in the British workplace: we're working too many hours.

Some people misinterpret the four-day week as a compressed hours four-day week, where workers work their normal amount of hours over four days rather than five. For example, a worker putting in 40 hours a week moves to doing 40 hours over four-days rather than five with four 10-hour days. I want to be absolutely clear on this – this is not what four-day week campaigners mean by a four-day week and there is a real danger of four very long working days exacerbating problems such as stress, overwork and burnout which a true reduced hour four-day week is seeking to address.

When human resources practitioners and wellbeing leads speak of mental health webinars, ping-pong tables and massages to improve wellbeing, the elephant in the room is always long working hours. The expectation to work a 9–5, five-day working week – and in many cases even more than that – puts way too much pressure on people and, in many ways, creates a society that sets itself up to fail. This model just doesn't allow enough time for everything else in life, especially for parents already struggling to juggle childcare responsibilities.

The fundamental question we need to ask ourselves here is: why is being busy and working all the time seen as a badge of honour in today's society? Until this changes, society will not be able to move en masse towards a shorter working week. But there are signs of hope this culture is beginning to shift and change.

In the UK, support for a four-day week with no loss of pay is higher than ever before with polling consistently showing more than two-thirds of the public behind it.[13] It's popular across the board but, when you break down the demographics, it's even more popular with Gen-Z and Millenials. The signs here are that younger generations do not want their lives to be defined by work in the same way they've seen it has been for their parents and grandparents' generations. The burgeoning number of viral social media posts on Instagram, Twitter and TikTok lamenting the amount of time we are forced to spend at work is further proof of this.

In Chapter Two we'll hear about the numerous pilots and trials that have taken place across the world. What they show is that a four-day week with no loss of pay can be a win–win for both workers and employers. There are many, many, many benefits including:

- Improved work–life balance: By working four days a week instead of the standard five, employees have more time for personal pursuits and family time, resulting in better work–life balance and reduced stress levels.
- Increased productivity: Research has shown that longer hours do not necessarily lead to increased productivity. In fact, working too many hours can result in burnout, reduced motivation and decreased productivity. A four-day week leads to increased productivity due to higher morale, improved job satisfaction and the ability to work more efficiently.

---

13. https://www.mirror.co.uk/news/politics/four-day-week-norm-uk-29861791

- Reduced carbon footprint: With one less day of commuting and energy consumption, a shorter working week can have a positive environmental impact.
- Increased employment opportunities: By shortening the working week, employers in some sectors may have to hire more staff to maintain current levels of productivity. This could potentially create new job opportunities and decrease unemployment rates.
- Better employee recruitment and retention: Offering a four-day week is an attractive perk for potential employees and increases job satisfaction and retention rates among current employees.

As campaigners for a four-day week, we often struggle to define our key messages as the myriad of benefits makes it difficult to choose the most popular. But this is a welcome problem to have. If implemented more widely across the economy, which we hope it eventually will be, there are many more ways in which society would benefit. One of the less talked about potential impacts would be greater gender equality as a result of men and women sharing paid and unpaid work, such as childcare, housework and caring responsibilities, more equally.

According to the Women's Budget Group[14], shorter working hours have been associated with a lower gender gap in unpaid hours of work, paid hours of work and wages. In England and Wales – 38 per cent of employed women

---

[14] https://wbg.org.uk/fgnd-blog/shorter-working-week/

work part time, compared with 13 per cent of men.[15] With men taking a greater share of domestic responsibilities, implementing a four-day week across society would mean women wouldn't have to keep missing out on career opportunities.

Dr Sara Reis, Deputy Director and Head of Policy and Research at the Women's Budget Group, said, *"We know that care is more evenly shared when men are working fewer paid hours. A shorter working week can lead to men being more involved in child-rearing and therefore distribute care more fairly between women and men."* She also gives a warning: *"If women are spending their extra time on domestic labour while men spend it relaxing, we'll never see parity in how we share care."*

On climate change, research has shown that a four-day week could reduce the UK's carbon footprint by up to 127 million tonnes per year, which is the equivalent of taking 27 million cars off the road – effectively the entire UK private car fleet. A report by environmental organisation Platform London found that a reduction in working hours correlates with more sustainable energy and household consumption, reductions in carbon-intensive commuting and would enable people to draw more value from 'low-carbon' activities such as rest, exercising or community-building. Essentially, if people have more time on their hands they will have more time to engage with living a more environmentally sustainable lifestyle.

[15.] https://www.ons.gov.uk/employmentandlabourmarket/peopleinwork/
employmentandemployeetypes/timeseries/yccw/lms

From 2008–2009, a large-scale experiment in the American State of Utah shifted most public-sector state employees to a four-day week to save energy and carbon.[16] The experiment showed that when eliminating Fridays as a work day, huge energy savings could be made by reducing the use of office lighting, elevator operating, heating or air conditioning.

Another study by independent think tank Autonomy found that by simply making Friday a day off, UK carbon emissions stemming from electricity production could drop by up to 24 per cent – reducing the entire energy sector's emissions by five per cent. Assuming a four-day week would effectively replace a workday with a weekend day, our energy consumption for that day could potentially reduce by 10 per cent and this lower electricity consumption combined with a lower carbon intensity of up to 15 per cent, could potentially lower emissions by as much as 24 per cent. Autonomy says this reduction in electricity use would be compounded by the amount of carbon-intensive commuting eliminated by a four-day week (or three-day weekend).

Reduced electricity use and fewer cars on the road would make a serious dent in our carbon footprint. Shorter working hours is one of the swiftest and easiest ways to take action on the climate. By simply working less, workers and companies can limit their environmental impact; and they don't need to sit around waiting for the Government to act.

To help with the cost of living, Autonomy also calculated potential savings to workers from reduced commuting and childcare costs that would arise from moving to a four-day,

---

[16.] https://www.scientificamerican.com/article/four-day-workweek-energy-environment-economics-utah/

32-hour working week with no loss of pay. They found that a parent with two children would save, on average, £3232.40 per year across both costs, or roughly £269.36 per month. A parent with one child would save £1789.40 on average per year across both costs, or roughly £150 per month.

A four-day week would also give people more time to volunteer in their local communities, care for loved ones and take part in local democracy. In many ways, this isn't dissimilar from what former Prime Minister David Cameron was advocating through his 'Big Society' mission. There were lots of problems with the 'Big Society' agenda and it never really came to full fruition, but communities taking back control over their lives would be eminently more possible under a four-day working week for all.

The 4 Day Week Campaign[17] is demanding that a four-day week becomes the normal way of working by the end of the decade. This may sound unrealistic but the public believe it is possible. According to polling by Survation in 2023, 58 per cent of the British public expect a four-day week to be the normal way of working by 2030, with only 22 per cent believing it won't. The polling also found that 65 per cent of the public support the Government exploring the introduction of a four-day week.

If you're not convinced by now, then remember that a new wave of technology could mean a four-day week is inevitable anyway. With more automation, new technology and artificial intelligence on the way, many have argued moving to a shorter working week will be a necessity for

---

[17] https://www.4dayweek.co.uk/

sharing a diminishing amount of work. The Nobel Prize winning economist Christopher Pissarides – a professor at the London School of Economics – said in 2023[18] that as a result of artificial intelligence: *"I'm very optimistic that we could increase productivity. We could increase our well-being generally from work and we could take off more leisure. We could move to a four-day week easily."* Rather than being scared of artificial intelligence taking our jobs, a shorter working week could allow us to embrace this new technology.

Workers, employers, the economy, our society and our environment all stand to benefit from a four-day week. With automation and artificial intelligence, it's probably inevitable anyway. But now let's turn to the evidence that it actually works in practice.

[18.] https://time.com/6268804/artificial-intelligence-pissarides-productivity/

1. https://labourlist.org/2020/11/four-day-working-week-demanded-as-18-million-days-lost-to-poor-mental-health/

2. The Evidence It Works

"When people enjoy having an extra day off, that creates better work–life balance which, in turn, makes people happier and less stressed. And happier people perform better at work."

Claire Daniels, CEO of Leeds-based digital marketing agency Trio Media

A growing number of four-day week experiments have taken place across the world over the last few years, primarily led by private-sector companies, governments and a few local authorities.

In 2022, we ran a UK pilot, the biggest to take place anywhere in the world so far. It was coordinated by the 4 Day Week Campaign, the think tank Autonomy and the not-for-profit 4 Day Week Global. I came up with the idea of running it after being challenged by a businessman when speaking on a panel at an event in London. He pointed out that there wasn't much evidence at the time that the four-day week could work in the UK. I had mentioned other countries that had tried it successfully, including Iceland, but he made a very valid point that this didn't necessarily mean the benefits would translate to the UK. I wanted to prove they would.

We launched the pilot in early January 2022 with coverage in the *Guardian* and a press release sent out to the rest of the media. To our astonishment, we were quickly inundated with over 500 companies registering their interest and signing up for online information sessions. In the end, 61 organisations and 2,900 workers participated.

The trial had extensive research support in place, led by Juliet Schor, Professor of Sociology at Boston College, and Brendan Burchell's team at the University of Cambridge. Speaking as the trial got underway, Professor Schor, who has since gone on to deliver a major TED talk making the case for a four-day week, said:

> *"I'm excited to be working on the research side for this historic trial. We'll be analysing how employees respond to having an extra day off, in terms of stress and burnout, job and life satisfaction, health, sleep, energy use, travel and many other aspects of life. The four-day week is generally considered to be a triple dividend policy – helping employees, companies, and the climate. Our research efforts will be digging into all of this."*

At the end of the trial, remarkably, [1] of the 61 companies that participated, at least 56 decided to continue with the four-day week, with 18 making the change permanent.

---

[1] https://autonomy.work/portfolio/uk4dwpilotresults/

One of the most exciting things about the trial was the wide variety of different sectors represented. From a local fish and chip shop in Norfolk to large corporates based in the City of London, participating sectors included:

- Education
- Workplace consultancy
- Banking
- Care
- Financial services
- IT software training;
- Professional development and legal training
- Housing
- Automotive supply services
- Online retail
- Sustainable homecare
- Skincare
- Animation studios
- Building and construction recruitment services
- Food and beverage and hospitality
- Digital marketing
- Comprehensive case management services for people recovering from traumatic injury

Of the 61 companies that took part, the largest sector represented was marketing/advertising, with eight firms (18 per cent). The second largest subset was professional services with seven (16 per cent), and charities/nonprofits made up the third largest group (11 per cent).

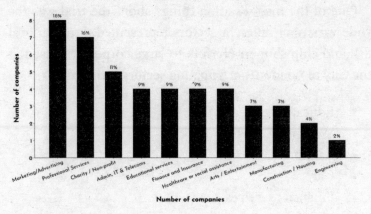

Figure 1: Participating companies by industry

While the employee size distribution was wide – with one company of around 1,000 staff – 66 per cent of firms had 25 or fewer employees and 22 per cent had 50 or more. A handful of companies had more than 250.

The full results of this groundbreaking pilot are best understood by dividing them into two parts: impact on the organisation and impact on workers. The results speak for themselves:

Organisational Performance

- The vast majority of companies were satisfied that business performance and productivity were maintained
- Companies' revenue stayed broadly the same, rising by 1.4 per cent on average from the beginning of the trial compared to the end. When compared with a comparable six-month period the year before,

revenues showed a much larger increase of 35 per cent on average

- There was a substantial decline (57 per cent) in the likelihood that an employee would quit, dramatically improving job retention
- The number of sick days fell by 65 per cent
- Companies reported an improved ability to hire new workers

Workers

- The well-being of workers dramatically improved, with stress and levels of burnout significantly declining. Before-and-after data showed 39 per cent of employees were less stressed and 71 per cent had reduced levels of burnout at the end of the trial
- Anxiety, fatigue and sleep problems decreased, while mental and physical health both improved
- Over the six-month trial period, measures of work–life balance improved. Respondents found it easier to balance their work with both family and social commitments and were more satisfied with their household finances, relationships and how their time was being managed.
- 60 per cent of employees found an increased ability to combine paid work with care responsibilities, and 62 per cent reported it was easier to combine work with social life

- There were significant reported improvements in life satisfaction
- In the trial, the time men spent looking after children increased by more than double that of women (from 27 per cent to 13 per cent), boosting gender equality

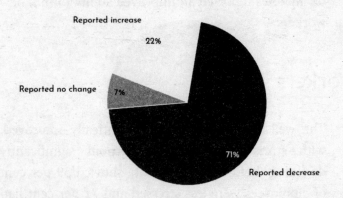

Figure 11: Change in participating employees' reported levels of 'burnout' between baseline and endpoint surveys. Employees were asked, using a 5 point frequency scale ('never' to 'always'), to grade how often they had experienced different markers of burnout ('exhaustion', 'frustration', etc.) in the preceding 4 weeks, from which a combined score was calculated.

For many employees taking part, the positive effects of a four-day week were worth more than their weight in money. Fifteen per cent of employees said that no amount of money would induce them to accept a five-day schedule over the four-day week to which they were now accustomed. Additionally, employee survey data found the impact on work intensity was barely noticeable. While there was a small increase in work intensity recorded for over a third of employees, 31 per cent believed it had declined and the remainder (33 per cent) saw no change.

For the five companies who weren't recorded as continuing at the end of the trial: one started late and was still in the pilot phase, another opted to try a four-and-a-half day week instead, and three opted for a total pause in their organisation. I had a long conversation with the manager of one of those three and the main problem they faced was that they had already been struggling with job recruitment prior to the trial and so weren't in the best place to try something new. However, all three organisations that opted for a total pause said they were open to coming back to the four-day week in the future. There were certainly no disasters in the experiment.

The overwhelmingly positive results of the UK pilot mirrored results seen in previous trials in Iceland, the USA, Ireland, New Zealand and Australia. As a result, many more companies are beginning to trial and adopt a four-day week – most notably Unilever in New Zealand and Australia, Panasonic in Japan, Bolt and Kickstarter in the USA and Atom Bank in the UK.

One of the first companies to test a four-day week was a New Zealand Financial Services company called Perpetual Guardian. After an initial six-month trial period which saw 240 staff move from a five-day to a four-day week without losing any pay, they recorded a 20 per cent increase in productivity, improvements in staff wellbeing and an increase in profits. *"This is an idea whose time has come,"* said Andrew Barnes, Perpetual Guardian's founder who is also the founder of 4 Day Week Global. *"We need to get more companies to give it a go. They will be surprised at the improvement in their company, their staff and in their wider community,"* he said.[2]

When Microsoft trialled a four-day week in Japan, productivity jumped by 40 per cent. When Atom Bank moved to a four-day week, job applications rose by 500 per cent in just three months. The potential benefits for companies are huge and it seems the early pioneers are reaping the rewards.

In the USA and Ireland, 4 Day Week Global ran another pilot in 2022 which involved 33 participating companies and over 900 employees.[3] Administrative, IT, and telecoms sectors comprised the largest section of the trial, with 12 in that category, then the second largest subset was professional services, with the third being non-profits. Once again, the results were a win–win for both workers and employers. Revenues went up, job recruitment improved and employees were extremely satisfied with their new way of life.

At the end of the trial, workers were asked a set of retrospective questions about their overall experience. On a 0–10 scale, where 0 was very bad and 10 was very good, the average score was 9.1, a very high level of satisfaction. When asked if they wanted to continue, almost every worker (97 per cent) said yes, they definitely did. Again, reassuringly, the change did not lead to an increase in the intensity or pace of work, on average, as measured from before the trial took place to the end of the trial.

---

[2] https://www.4dayweek.com/research-perpetual-guardians-4day-workweek-trial-qualitative-research-analysis

[3] https://www.4dayweek.com/us-ireland-results

Another study by Henley Business School[4], published in 2019, on the growing four-day week trend found that of those businesses who have already adopted it, nearly two-thirds have reported improvements in staff productivity. The research also found an increase in quality of life for employees, with over three quarters (78 per cent) of businesses that had implemented the change saying staff were happier. Seventy per cent of staff were less stressed and 62 per cent took fewer sick days. Almost two thirds (63 per cent) of employers said that providing a four-day week had helped them attract and retain talent. Nearly half (46 per cent) of larger businesses surveyed, said making the switch will be important for future business success.

Alongside these campaigner-organised private-sector initiatives, a number of government schemes have got off the ground too. In Scotland, Spain and Portugal, government-led trials are either already or about to get underway in both the private and public sectors. Belgium became the first country to introduce national legislation with a new law coming into force in February 2022 giving workers the right to decide whether they work their hours over four days or five. This is essentially a compressed-hours four-day week, which as I've already said we're not advocating for, but given that Belgium works fewer hours on average than the UK already, this is a major step in the right direction.

The United Arab Emirates (UAE) has also cut its working week to four and a half days. *"The UAE is the first nation in*

---

[4] https://www.henley.ac.uk/news/2019/four-day-week-pays-off-for-uk-business

the world to introduce a national working week shorter than the global five-day week," it said.

Public Sector

The largest public sector shorter working week trials to date took place in Iceland. Again, they were an 'overwhelming success.' From 2015–2019, Iceland ran two large-scale trials of a reduced working week of 35–36 hours with no reduction in pay. The results were analysed in a joint project by the UK think tank Autonomy and the research organisation Association for Sustainability and Democracy (Alda) in Iceland[1].

The analysis of the results – which included 2,500 workers (over one per cent of Iceland's entire working population) – demonstrated the transformative positive effects of a shorter working week for both employees and businesses:

- Productivity and service provision remained the same or improved across most trial workplaces
- Worker wellbeing dramatically increased across a range of indicators, from perceived stress and burnout, to health and work-life balance
- The trials remained revenue neutral for both the city council and the government, providing a crucial, and so far largely overlooked blueprint of how future trials might be organised around the world

One of the trials was conducted in the capital, Reykjavík, by the city authorities. Starting from just two workplaces with a few dozen workers, it was expanded to more than

2,000 employees. Following the trial's success, Icelandic trade unions and their confederations achieved permanent reductions in working hours for tens of thousands of their members nationally. In total, 86 per cent of Iceland's entire working population has now either moved to working shorter hours or gained the right to shorten their working hours.

Will Stronge, Director of Research at Autonomy, commented at the time:

> *"This study shows that the world's largest ever trial of a shorter working week in the public sector was by all measures an overwhelming success. It shows that the public sector is ripe for being a pioneer of shorter working weeks – and lessons can be learned for other governments.*
>
> *Iceland has taken a big step towards the four-day working week, providing a great real-life example for Local Councils and those in the UK public sector considering implementing it here in the UK."*

First UK Council Trial

In January 2023, South Cambridgeshire District Council became the first UK council to trial a four-day week, reducing the hours of desk-based staff to 30 per week with no loss of pay for three months.

After three months, the trial was deemed so successful that an extension of a further year for office-based staff was approved, alongside a three-month trial for the Facilities Management team and Shared Waste services.

According to the Bennett Institute for Public Policy at the University of Cambridge, who analysed the results[5], performance was broadly maintained over the three-month period. Nine out of 16 performance areas monitored showed substantial improvement and the Institute noted that not a single area fell to a concerning performance level during the trial. The council also managed to save £760,000 for taxpayers through reduced spend on agency staff[2]. Survey data collected by the council showed the trial was overwhelmingly positive for staff's health and wellbeing.

The council decided to undertake the trial because of the acute recruitment and retention issues it was facing – mirrored across the public sector nationally; we'll hear more about the impact this is having on the NHS in Chapter Four. According to the Local Government Association, nine in ten councils across the UK are struggling with job retention and recruitment.[6] Before the trial started, South Cambridgeshire District Council was spending almost £2 million a year on agency staff, often in specialist roles where the private sector pays more. The Council predicted this bill could be halved if all the agency posts were filled permanently. Although the three-month trial wasn't expected to see much improvement in recruitment, as there was no guarantee it would continue, the Council's annual wage bill decreased by over £300,000 after just three months with fewer expensive agency fees being charged. Additionally, job posts which had been

[5] https://scambs.moderngov.co.uk/ieListDocuments.aspx?MId=9590&x=1

[6] https://www.localgov.co.uk/Nine-in-10-councils-experiencing-staffing-issues/55468

left empty for years were suddenly filled and some staff decided to stay at the council when they may have otherwise moved-on.

Prior to the trial taking place, the council outlined how, for more than a year, it had only been able to fill around eight out of every ten, or fewer, of its vacancies. Not being able to fill vacant posts – or using agency staff to cover them – is not only expensive but also disruptive. For example, when case officers change during planning applications, context and institutional memory can be lost, causing delays and frustration. The combination of reduced agency spends and improved recruitment during the three-month trial is a positive indication of what the Council hopes to see in the year-long trial: saving costs whilst maintaining high quality public services.

At the time of writing, another 18 councils have been in touch with the 4 Day Week Campaign to say they are actively considering running their own trials.

Long-term Benefits

One of the questions I'm often asked is about whether the benefits of adopting a four-day week last. Can the benefits be sustained once the novelty wears off? It's a fair question. If everyone is trying really hard during a six-month trial to make the four-day week work, surely those benefits will wear off further down the line? New research published in 2023 suggests not.

The most comprehensive study on this, again by 4 Day Week Global[7], looked for the first time at company and employee data a year on from trials that took place in the US, Canada, the UK and Ireland.

They found that a year after launching trials, employees' average working hours continued to fall as a result of workers continuing to operate more efficiently. Staff retention had also risen from around 70 to more than 90 per cent. This backs up anecdotal evidence from our network of accredited four-day week employers in the UK, where a number of companies signed up have been operating under four-day weeks for over five years, and in a few cases over a decade.

In summary, the evidence clearly shows that the four-day week with no loss of pay works. It seems that every time a trial takes place, six months later we hear it's been an overwhelming success. The evidence is clear: after numerous trials, pilots and case studies across the world, the four-day working week is a tried and tested success. Now let's find out how to implement it.

---

[7] https://www.4dayweek.com/press-releases/working-hours-continue-to-fall

1. https://autonomy.work/portfolio/icelandsww/

2. https://www.scambs.gov.uk/your-council-and-democracy/four-day-working-week-trial/

3. Different Approaches and Models to Implementation

"If you can do this in a small production environment, it demonstrates that the five-day week is a construct and something that could have been gotten rid of a long time ago."

Sam Smith, Founder of Pressure Drop Brewery in London

The huge potential benefits to workers' wellbeing and life outside of work that arise from implementing the four-day week should now be clear and fairly easy to understand. For many progressive bosses, this is enough to be persuaded to make the jump, as for the type of boss that believes strongly in their staff's wellbeing, giving something back feels really important. Of course, they also need to have enough confidence it won't jeopardise the business. For many small businesses and other organisations struggling to afford inflation-match pay rises – a particular issue we've seen over the last year with inflation so high – the four-day week with no loss of pay is another way of giving back to staff.

However, the shorter working week's potential positive impact on organisational performance is the most important part to many business owners. This is driven by a number of factors as discussed in the previous chapter. In order to at least maintain the level of output and quality of service in fewer working hours, the business in question is required to change the way tasks are *organised*, *distributed* and *executed*. How this change is carried out will depend on the approach taken. Below are two competing strategies for companies to successfully implement the changes needed for a viable shorter working week in both a trial and beyond. The pros and cons of both are discussed, providing important context for deciding which approach would best suit your work setting.

Productivity Driven: The 100-80-100 Model

One of the driving factors in making the business case for a four-day week has been its ability to substantially improve productivity. From numerous studies, cited throughout the book so far, trials of shorter-working-week practices have demonstrated how output and business performance can not only be maintained in fewer hours but in some cases even improved. We have seen various explanations for how a shorter working week without a loss in pay can improve productivity: staff feeling better rested and more focused on the job at hand, or increased time off from work having a positive impact on reducing sickness. But the new working pattern also forces organisations to rethink some of their working practices that may not be creating 'value' for the business. For example, the amount of time staff spend in meetings is often the first thing to be reviewed when shorterworkingweek practices are implemented. The question that follows is this: Do the positive impacts of a shorter working week occur as a natural outcome of switching to this model or is there a guiding approach that businesses follow when preparing to do so?

For many organisations taking part in four-day week trials around the world, the answer has been the latter, with a specific approach geared towards improving productivity and changing the business focus towards output rather than hours worked. This strategy is often referred to as the 100-80-100 model: 100% pay for 80% of the time with a commitment to maintain 100% output. This strategy was designed and implemented by the New Zealand business owner and entrepreneur Andrew Barnes when carrying out a four-day week trial in 2018.[1] Since then, Barnes and fellow entrepreneur Charlotte Lockhart have founded the consultancy service 4 Day Week Global which supports organisations looking to trial a four-day week. The 100-80-100 model operates by making time a 'scarce resource'. It poses the workforce a challenge to deliver their

---

[1.] Andrew Barnes company Perpetual Guardian carried out a four day week trial in 2018 that pioneered the 100-80-100 model. The trial was analysed by academics from the University of Auckland and Auckland University of Technology.

current productivity in four days rather than five. The idea is to provide staff with the opportunity to raise productivity and reduce operating costs by addressing their own behaviour. Staff are encouraged to assess their working day in order to find individual processes that could be a hindrance in preventing them from achieving their productivity targets and enjoying a four-day week. With every member of the team adopting this mindset, the intended outcome is an increase in productive output that can offset the extra free time 'gifted' to employees.

An approach such as the 100-80-100 model can be beneficial in a number of ways for certain organisations looking to trial or implement a four-day week. Firstly, if the work setting in question already has clearly defined Key Performance Indicators (KPIs) where productive outcomes can be easily quantified, it is likely staff within such organisations will be geared towards an outcomes-based approach. It can also be a viable strategy for businesses where performance evaluation is highly centred on the individual rather than the collective. Again, staff in such workplaces will already be more adaptive and proactive in adopting an outcomes-focused approach. Lastly, a productivity-focused approach can be conducive to organisations largely doing project, research or admin-based work. This is due to the work's 'elasticity' and consequent scope for productivity improvements. For example, certain project-based or admin tasks can be automated or made more efficient by improving the process or simplifying decision-making.

However, there are limitations to this approach that might not make it the right fit for every organisation. In workplaces where individual performance is difficult to quantify, such as a factory, a productivity-focused approach could well put pressure on individuals, creating higher levels of stress with adverse effects on both well-being and performance, the very thing you are trying to improve. Service- or sales-based tasks are often less open to being automated or made more efficient due to the work value being derived less by the process, but more by its stated outcome. For example, a sales assistant needs to maximise opportunities for making sales in order to hit pre-established targets. However, this is not to say that certain sectors or jobs are not conducive to shorterworkingweek practices, but rather that not all approaches will work for every industry.

Organisational Prioritisation: The 'Fitness' Approach

While the drive to improve productivity has been an important strategy in building the business case for a four-day week, it's important to remember that moving to a shorter working week can also address long-standing structural issues. One such strategy aims at using the four-day week as a tool that allows organisations to reassess their overall mission and what they are trying to achieve. The business owner and American entrepreneur, Banks Benitez[2], refers to this approach as one of 'fitness,' whereby the four-day week

---

[2] For more insight into Banks Benitez's ideas on prioritisation and the four-day work week see his conversation on the Greg McKeown podcast: https://podcasts. apple.com/us/podcast/banks-benitez-on-the-magic-of-the-4-day-workweek/ id1513285647?i=1000496897595

is achieved by reprioritising the most important work. For Benitez, whose work is covered in more detail in Chapter Six, the fitness element of the four-day week refers to it not simply being a one-off decision, but a process that requires regular effort and consideration. This strategy aims to take the focus of successfully implementing a four-day week away from individuals and instead hold organisational leadership accountable. Essentially, rather than finding time savings by increasing individual output, a fitness approach focuses on *evaluating organisational input*.

In practice, this means an organisation reevaluates its strategic priorities by assessing how certain services contribute towards achieving its goals or 'mission,' deciding which working practices offer the most in terms of 'value' and creating team collaboration where staff availability is most advantageous to cultivate client or stakeholder relationships. This type of approach can help organisations that evaluate performance on a more qualitative team basis, such as charities and NGOs. It can also be advantageous for smaller organisations where decision-making is less hierarchical and conducted more collegiately.

However, just like the 100-80-100 model, there are drawbacks to this approach. For companies that offer services tied to government or core funding contracts, it can be difficult to deprioritise particular streams of work or reorganise services that adhere to strict KPIs.

When deciding which strategy to adopt for your organisation it's important to remember that the two are not mutually exclusive; you can take principles and approaches from both. The most important thing for senior leaders to remember when devising an implementation strategy is to be clear-headed when setting up a trial, and recognise that achieving success depends to a large extent on the buy-in and ownership staff feel they have over the trial process. By considering this first, you will have a better idea of which strategy will be most feasible from an operational perspective and motivate staff to implement the changes needed to make the four-day week viable in both the short and long term.

Five Models of Implementation

It's important to state there is no one-size-fits-all approach to implementing a four-day week. From various trials, we have seen it applied in many different ways that take into consideration both the desires of staff and operational feasibility. Below are the five main models for implementing a 'four-day' or shorter working week.

1. Fifth Day Stoppage

This is the most obvious and commonplace adoption of a four-day week where a company simply shuts down operations for one additional day per week. This is by far the easiest and most straightforward model to adopt, if feasible, and is very common in office-based jobs where the office can be shut on the same day each week. Friday tends to be the most popular as workers can benefit from a three-day weekend. Then Monday is still the first day back in the office when everyone catches up as everyone does now. Anecdotally, there seems to be something transformational that takes place from a workers' well-being perspective when they have three days off in a row each week, so we recommend this model if possible for your organisation. Everyone loves a bank holiday weekend when they get to enjoy three days off work in a row. Just imagine how that would feel every week.

Example: A video game studio opted for a fifth-day stoppage because it was important for staff to be present at the same time for collaboration. After polling staff on preferences, the studio decided to shut down on Fridays. We've found this to be a popular choice in companies where staff collaboration is more important than five-day coverage.

2. Staggered

Staff take alternating days off: for example, all staff may be divided into two teams, with one taking Mondays off, and the other taking Fridays. This is a popular choice in companies where five-day coverage is important.

Example: A digital marketing agency organised its staggered days off using a 'buddy' system. Staff members with similar knowledge and skills pair up. The partners alternate their day off, in order to ensure five-day coverage of key functions.

3. Decentralised

Different departments operate on different work patterns, possibly resulting in a mixture of the two models above. This may also incorporate other arrangements, such as some staff working a four-day equivalent over five shorter working days. A decentralised model is sometimes chosen in companies whose departments have highly contrasting functions and challenges.

Example: A housing association, which includes departments specialising in everything from administration to community outreach and building repairs, opted for this model. Each department was asked to take the lead in devising a four-day week model fit for its own purposes.

Another Example: A media organisation which has to be on call and ready to respond 24/7 opted for this model because, unfortunately for them, the news doesn't stop on a Friday (or even at the weekend)! This meant staff rotated their days off to ensure five-day coverage, including a weekend on-call system. Staff reported this system worked very well for them as workers felt more refreshed and better able to deal with media enquiries on the days they were working, and, due to the immediate nature of the media requests handled, there wasn't much handover of work anyway.

4. Annualised

This is where staff work a 32-hour average working week, calculated on the scale of a year. This works well for some organisations and means that sometimes staff will be working a normal five-day week or perhaps even longer, but at other times they will be working fewer days. This can work well for organisations driven by project-based work where staff can be really busy when delivering a specific project, but a lot less busy at other times.

Example: A restaurant whose business is highly seasonal opted to pilot an annualised four-day week, with longer opening times in summer compensated by shorter opening times in winter.

Another example: At an events management company, staff work for five, six or even seven days a week in the intense periods where they are really busy preparing for and running events. For the rest of the year, when things are less busy, they work a four-day week or less, averaging out as a 32-hour working week across the year.

It's important to remember that overtime and time off in lieu under a four-day week system works the same way it always has under a five-day week. Under all of these models, there may be weeks where, for whatever reason, staff need to work all five or even more days. As long as they are getting those days back added to their annual leave allowance, then you can still apply the four-day week model.

5. Conditional

Staff entitlement to the four-day week is tied to ongoing performance monitoring. Seniors in the company may decide to temporarily suspend the four-day week for certain departments or individuals, if there is evidence staff are failing to meet agreed performance targets. This may lead to uneven situations where some staff/departments continue to work five days at times.

Example: A company adopting a decentralised model required each department to agree on a set of KPIs that would need to be met, in order to retain a four-day week. This meant some departments and individuals entered the pilot later than others, and some were temporarily suspended from the four-day week during a six-month pilot period.

We would recommend trying to avoid using this model if possible, as it can lead to resentment among staff.

Sometimes these five models can overlap. For example, a company could have an 'annualised' four-day week, on a 'staggered' pattern, or have a 'decentralised' model, involving a 'conditional' element. There is also the option to implement on a department-by-department basis, rather than attempting to move the entire organisation across in one go. This can ease the pressure on HR departments and be a good test bed for the rest of the organisation.

The total amount of weekly hours you choose to implement needs some consideration too. This largely depends on how many hours you are coming down from. For organisations where full-time workers are putting in 40 hours a week, the jump to 32 could be quite steep so you may want to consider coming down more gradually to 35 or 34 hours in the first instance. Conversely, for organisations where full-time workers are already putting in 35 hours a week – which is quite common in the public sector for example – you may want to reduce further to maybe 30 or even 28 hours. We do see this quite a lot and there are many four-day week organisations that have opted to reduce their hours this far.

Pressure Drop Brewery

Pressure Drop Brewery in Tottenham, London, has been selling craft beers for ten years. As part of a qualitative research project on the UK pilot, we spoke to one of its founders, who started the business with hopes of differentiating it from bigger, more growth-focused operations. A founding principle of the company was to 'create jobs that fit around our lives.'

"We're a bit more mellow-paced. When we started the business we wanted to change the way we worked," said the founder.

The current manager became interested in the four-day week because he hoped the brewery *"could become a leader in something positive."* He also found it consistent with its broader ambition to reduce its carbon footprint through investments in green energy. Being in manufacturing, he feels he has a point to prove.

The manager said: *"If you can do this in a small production environment, it demonstrates that the five-day week is a construct and something that could have been gotten rid of a long time ago."*

How were they going to make it work? The brewery adopted a staggered four-day week model in order to maintain production over five days. The plan was to split the production team into two groups, with one taking Monday off and the other Friday (swapping each month).

Staff also told us about the significant preparation period before the pilot. As part of the lead-in, the brewers studied their brewing process closely: breaking down the tasks involved, running their phone timers in their pockets, searching for new efficiencies and developing a new set of production targets. One brewer described an atmosphere of excitement, solidarity and challenge around finding ways to reduce working time:

"It's like cooking a huge Sunday roast, trying to get everything to finish at the same time."

A phrase we heard a lot in our conversations with staff was 'mucking in.' On days when not everyone was present, staff could be required to jump in on tasks that may have previously been outside their remit, helping with brewing, packaging, or picking up the phone. The staff we interviewed celebrated the sharing of skills and the sense of collective effort involved. The manager said, *"The whole team now does what the manager does,"* by forecasting busy periods and identifying what needs attention. When we asked him whether he was worried about work becoming more intense, he said they were busier, but less stressed:

"Being busy doesn't make you stressed, being out of control is what makes you stressed... We want to be more busy, less stressed. I don't like being bored at work, I like it when there's an atmosphere of things happening... If we're busy it means there is a lot of beer going out of the door and things are going well."

. . .

First Step: Persuading the Board

Persuading the board or senior figures of a company to adopt a four-day week is always a necessary first step. After all, these are the people that ultimately make the key decisions around working conditions, even if the demands have come from the shop floor. As you saw in Chapter Two, there is an abundance of evidence to show the four-day week with no loss of pay works, and we know it has already been successfully implemented across various different sectors and organisations. Most people think of the policy as something adopted primarily for the benefit of workers, but there is actually a very strong business case that can be deployed to persuade the board it is a route to improved performance and greater growth.

Firstly, a four-day week stimulates innovation. The statistics are quite clear that many people who work a five-day week feel overworked, with one in four sick days a direct result of overwork.[3] When workers are better rested, they are more able to think creatively and come up with new ideas. The UK trial saw a significant decline in stress and burnout for employees, with an overall 65% reduction in absenteeism.[4] Positive mental health at work allows workers to think more clearly and innovatively.

This extra rest then translates into increased productivity. Trials by big companies such as Microsoft in Japan saw productivity increase by 40%, and the UK trial showed productivity and business performance either increased or remained consistent, with 55% of employees reporting increased ability at work. This boost in productivity often leads to higher revenue and profit. A four-day week can definitely help businesses save money. Shifting to a

---

[3.] https://www.huffingtonpost.co.uk/entry/our-fetishisation-of-overwork_uk_5bfecea0e4b0efd3f1ffe911

[4.] https://autonomy.work/wp-content/uploads/2023/02/The-results-are-in-The-UKs-four-day-week-pilot.pdf

four-day week can save on utilities like rent, electricity and energy consumption. In November 2021, another study by Henley Business School found that businesses saved around 2.2% of their total turnover.[5]

A four-day week also makes it easier for employers to attract and retain talented employees. Given today's tight labour market, this is perhaps the strongest argument for persuading the board. We know the policy is popular with workers and that firms adopting it have seen a surge in job applications. Similarly, a four-day week is a tangible incentive to improve job retention; reducing costs and disruption. One of the main motivators for employers participating in the UK trial was to gain a competitive advantage in the labour market. Several managers had reported difficulties retaining staff after Covid. This was compounded by quiet quitting, the 'great resignation' and a greater desire for above-inflation salary increases. During the UK trial, resignations dropped by 57% overall and 63% of businesses found it easier to attract and retain talent.

Finally, perhaps the most overlooked aspect of the business case for a four-day week is that it enhances employers' reputation as ethical and innovative. Shorter working hours can be positioned as part of your strategy to reduce your carbon footprint, alongside sending a signal that the organisation treats employees well, caring for their wellbeing and recognising their responsibilities outside of work, as well as giving something back to the community.

[5.] https://www.henley.ac.uk/the-four-day-week#:~:text=The%20four%2Dday%20 week%20saves,saving%20£18%2C000%20each%20year

As we can see, there is a very convincing business case demonstrating that the four-day week is good for executives as well as workers. But the process of board approval requires more than just highlighting the many business benefits. It requires clarification, reassurances and clear explanations as to why only a four-day week can achieve these benefits.

One of the many perceived risks of running a shorter working week trial concerns maintaining organisational performance when there is a loss in working time. It is therefore vital to communicate to sceptical board members, shareholders and staff that the culture you are transitioning to will focus more on output and organisational performance than hours spent working. This requires a shift to output-focused working, which is covered in more detail in Chapter Six, but essentially requires an organisation to apply the majority of available labour to the real drivers of results, to achieve the same outcome in a shorter time frame. The four-day week is not about working harder, it's about working smarter – to sustain productivity levels in a shorter time frame. This is evident in the productivity measures we have already discussed, which show that those who work a four-day week are almost always just as – if not more – productive, because they begin to work smarter.

This inevitably leads to arguments that it would be more prudent to simply work smarter, find these efficiencies and then cut 20% of the workforce, saving large amounts on labour costs while maintaining performance. This would be a crucial miscalculation, which, in reality, would play out quite differently. Firstly, it is the promise of an extra day off that incentivises workers to maintain productivity levels. Secondly, the benefits of that increased rest are what provides the physical and mental capacity to sustain those productivity increases over a longer period of time.

If, however, you were simply to cut the workforce by 20%, you would see a negative effect on productivity, with staff morale and motivation diminishing with the corresponding increases to their workload. This would then be detrimental to health and wellbeing, with the likely result being an increase in absenteeism, presenteeism and turnover in staff.

Despite this, moral objections may still exist. One primary concern may be that the board cannot justify paying staff for five days when they are only working four. Employers may feel they are making a loss. However, as we can see from the numerous trials that have taken place all over the world, they are not. Productivity is almost always maintained and in many cases has actually increased. Workers are better rested, allowing them to be more focused, efficient and innovative and this is backed up by those who have reported an ability to perform better in their roles once they have transitioned to a four-day week. This is also partly down to workers becoming more motivated. But by pure productivity, revenue and staff turnover metrics, employers often make a net gain by reducing working hours.

Of course, the board will also have practical concerns that will need to be addressed and answered. We have already seen how to deal with some of these, such as how parts of the business that need to be maintained across the whole week can remain operational. Chapter Four will build on this, exploring how to address typical challenges around contracts, annual leave and other HR-related issues.

4. Typical Challenges

"When you're refreshed and rejuvenated – those are the times when I find myself enjoying teaching most. As the term goes on, you just get worn down by the long hours. A shorter working week would make my best teaching more sustainable. You'd have happier teachers who'd be in a better place to do their jobs and keep them in the profession for longer."

Chloe Tomlinson, a primary school teacher in South London

Part-Time Workers

Including part-time workers can be the issue that takes the most time to grapple with, so let's tackle that first. The time and energy needed to work out a solution here really depends on how many part-time workers you have. For organisations with only a small number, it shouldn't be a major sticking point.

The most important thing is to speak to everyone and come to a solution which works for as many part-timers as possible. Here are the most common solutions:

- Increase their pay (if feasible).
- Reduce part-time hours in line with reductions for full-time staff.
- Adjust annual leave entitlement to recognise the large uplift created by a four-day week.
- Allow part-time staff to accrue extra days/time off. For example, you could permit part-time staff to accrue hours in such a way that they would be entitled to a half-day off every two weeks or one day a month (depending on the number of days/hours they work). This option can also be incorporated into any active flexitime working policy.
- A combination of the above.

In a few rare cases, part-time workers have been excluded from the policy. This is easier to make the case for during a trial period than when a decision is being taken to make the move permanent. However, this is not recommended because you will almost certainly run into contractual issues further down the line if/when you decide to update contracts, and there is a real danger of alienating part-time workers.

Annual Leave

It is fairly common but not always the case that during any trial period – whether three months, six months or longer – holiday allowances stay the same. When the policy is implemented permanently, again some organisations have chosen to retain the same holiday allowance, but they are often reduced in line with the overall reduction in working hours. For example, those dropping from a full-time five-day week to four would see their holiday allowance reduced by 20 per cent.

This is seen as a fair option given that workers will be getting an extra day off each week with no reduction in pay. When workers come to book time off to go away on holiday, they already have an extra day a week they no longer need to take out of their annual leave allocation.

Bank Holidays

Many companies choose to put a new policy in place whereby bank holidays (which most commonly fall on a Monday) are treated as that week's non-working day (switching from Friday).

Other options are:

- A three-day week during bank holiday weeks
- Adding bank holidays to annual leave entitlement, allowing staff to choose when to take them

Billable Hours

Billable hours can act as a block to implementing the four-day week in certain sectors – the legal sector being one obvious example – because when firms charge their clients by the hour they could risk losing a substantial amount of income if charging for 32 hours per week instead of 40.

However, organisations we've worked with have been able to successfully get around this issue by:

- Moving partly or wholly from hourly billing to value-based or project-based fixed-fee billing

- Finding efficiencies within the billable-hour structure to deliver work in less time
- Maintaining billable hours by finding sufficient efficiencies in their non-billable overheads
- Some combination of the above

This may not be possible in all sectors but a conversation is certainly long overdue about moving away from the billable-hours model.

Contractual Changes

During a trial period, employment contracts are almost always left as they are and the four-day week is seen as a gift to employees, usually through a more informal opt-in agreement (see later in this chapter for an example). When making the decision to move permanently to a four-day week, there are two options:

- Rewrite employment contracts to recognise the reduction in weekly hours and the new four-day working pattern. You may want to seek legal advice from an employment lawyer on this
- Leave contracts as they are and keep the four-day week more informally in place through an opt-in agreement that can be renewed every year

Not Every Staff Member Buying-in

There tends to be at least one grumpy employee at most organisations who just loves working a five-day week. Some people are set in their ways and resistant to change, even if it's in their own interests. If this is the case, you can try to persuade them with all the arguments we've set out, but if they're still making your life difficult by not budging, you could let them continue working five days a week, but with no extra pay. If this is in an office environment where you are running a full shutdown, they will probably need to work from home on the fifth day as you will want to make sure you still benefit from the energy savings of being closed for an extra day.

Do what you can to try and persuade them of the benefits, and try to highlight how other staff members are benefiting, but in our experience, some people just aren't ready to embrace having an extra day of free time each week. Allowing these types of people to still work five days, but with no extra pay, is the best way forward.

Staff Taking on Extra Work on Their Day Off

With the cost of living crisis, we have heard some rare stories of staff using their extra day off to take on more work. In terms of rest and wellbeing, this obviously defeats the point of a four-day week but the reality is that for some people this will be really important to give them extra financial security.

To avoid this, one organisation mandated their staff not to take up additional work on their day off but in reality, this is a hard thing to do and we would recommend consulting an employment lawyer if you are planning to.

In general, we've not heard many cases of this happening but it's understandable that it does during a cost of living crisis so it could be something to consider.

Self-employed and Zero-hours Contracts

Many self-employed people already have the freedom to work a four-day week. However, for self-employed and zero-hours contract workers on low incomes who can't afford to lose a day's money – we need to see wider policy changes implemented across the economy. For example: a higher living wage, a ban on zero-hours contracts and an extension of workers' rights. Ultimately, implementing a four-day week with no loss in pay across PAYE sectors should put upward pressure on legally and socially accepted wages in all sectors.

It is common for people to say that the four-day week just doesn't work for people on any kind of temporary, insecure contract but I would argue this is the wrong way round. Insecure contracts such as zero-hours contracts are an inherent problem as they make implementing any kind of worker benefit very difficult. This problem is not directly caused by the four-day week but does mean millions of workers won't necessarily be able to benefit straight away.

How a Shorter Working Week Impacts Flexible Work Policies More Generally

When moving to a shorter working week there can be some concern over losing flexibility in order to accommodate a reduction in hours. However, this doesn't need to be the case and in general, most organisations trialling a shorter working week are looking to increase staff flexibility, rather than reduce it.

Example Opt-in agreement for shorter working week trial

Staff participation

All staff members, full time and part time can participate in the pilot. This form represents an 'Opt-in agreement' during the pilot which means that staff members can choose whether or not they would like to participate in the shorter working week (SWW) pilot. Staff members can also choose to opt out at any point during the pilot if they feel that it is not working for them (for whatever reason).

Additionally, if there is a significant issue with a particular staff member's performance during the pilot, it will be within the scope of the line manager in the performance management process to return to their original contracted hours for that staff member. In general staff will be encouraged to highlight early if they are facing any challenges with the pilot or anything else work related and discuss them with their line manager to address them before performance management issues arise.

Staff members will communicate their non-working day or hours to line manager (through 1-1s) and the team through a team calendar so that everyone aware of people's work patterns.

Working time during the pilot

For the period of the pilot we will institute **core office hours** i.e. when everybody is expected to be available for meetings (virtually or in-person), these core hours will be 10am-3pm on Tuesdays and Thursdays.

There may also be **surge times** of 'spikes' in activity or an important event/meeting scheduled for a day when a team member might not be working. Where possible, the SWW will be accommodated during surge periods (i.e. forward planning so that there is no need to work 5 days a week at the last minute) but it may be necessary for team members to be flexible and work a 5 day/37 hour week that week. If this is necessary, staff members who have worked an extra day can claim back TOIL in the following two weeks (see section on TOIL).

Annual leave and bank holidays

Annual leave will be on a Pro rata basis i.e. staff working a 28 hour week will receive 80% of the normal annual leave quota (20 days instead of 25 days).

Annual Leave can be alternatively calculated in hours: 1 day would be 7 hours, 1.5 days (10.5 hours).

As we are transitioning to a 28 hour week, staff that opt-in to the 28 hour week would lose1 day in annual leave in 2019, and 1.5 days in 2020. If the 28 hour week is continued past the end of, staff leave for 2020 would be further reduced by 3.5 days.

Accumulated days of annual leave will be added on as normal (e.g. team members who have earned an extra day annual leave for a year of completed service).

Bank holidays will be calculated pro rata basis - staff will take 7 bank holidays. For most weeks when a bank holiday falls, a staff member would have an extra day (or 7 hours) off – this would always be the Monday of the Bank Holiday unless that was the staff member's normal day off anyway, in which case the staff member could take a different day off that week.. For staff members working a 28 hour week over 5 days and don't normally work a full day on the Monday – they would take the Monday off as Bank Holiday and then take the remaining 'bank holiday hours' at some point that week. Once a year, all staff participating in the 28-hour week will work on the Bank Holiday. Each staff member would work the equivalent of 28 hours that week rather and this can be done on any day of the week, including the Bank Holiday itself.

Time Off In Lieu (TOIL)

TOIL will be taken as normal and all TOIL requests will be discussed and agreed with line managers.
During surge times if members to work a 37 hour week, they can take TOIL for that 5th day worked (or extra 7 hours worked) within the following 2 weeks.
When travelling at the weekend, TOIL can be requested for the days worked.
If working in the evenings whilst travelling, staff can take TOIL for hours worked. If a staff member is travelling but not actively working in the evenings, the staff member does not accrue TOIL.

Team meetings will be used as an opportunity to identify if there are obvious days in coming two months when the team need to be working, so that staff can plan ahead.

Staff Contracts and Organisational Policy

These will not be amended during the pilot as this is a temporary change to working hours. If we decide to implement the 28 hour week on a more permanent basis then we would update staff contracts.

Only following a thorough review of the pilot after it has finished will staff, in consultation with the Board, determine whether the 28 hour week will be made policy. Only then will a policy be developed and staff contracts changed.

Monitoring Plan

In addition to staff M&E tools listed below we also hope to work with an external evaluator who can help us conduct our staff surveys and interviews so that staff can be as open as possible about their experiences and to help us more objectively review the outcomes of the pilot.

We plan to monitor the 28 hour week week in the following ways:
1. **Personal monitoring and reflection.**
2. **An anonymous survey**
3. **Personal objectives**
4. **Check-in discussions**
5. **Operational Reports to the Board and Logframe (in December and April)** –
6. **End Review Interviews**.

If you wish to participate in the pilot under the conditions stated above, please sign and date the opt-in agreement below.

Name................................

Signature

....

Date

....

Before heading into a trial it is important to ensure staff are clear about current flexible work policies (particularly time off in lieu), flexitime and working from home policies) so they can align with the new working schedule. For many organisations, these policies are carried out on an informal basis. The move to a shorter working week provides the ideal opportunity to reevaluate these policies and make sure they align with the demands the four-day week will impose on contact time between teams, and work potentially being carried out in non-scheduled time.

More Challenging Sectors for Implementation

It should be very clear already that there is no one-size-fits-all approach to implementing the four-day week. Implementation will vary from sector to sector. An office-based company moving to a four-day week will look very different to a brewery or a fish and chip shop, for example.

We know many companies across various different sectors have made it work, with successful outcomes for employers and employees. However, speaking from experience there are certain sectors where implementation is more challenging. The problems a four-day week seeks to solve vary from sector to sector.

To give a specific example, employees in the construction sector report some of the highest work-related physical and mental health problems, most of which are intimately connected to overwork. Construction workers currently put in over five hours more per week than the average worker in

Britain. A shorter working week could make construction significantly more attractive to prospective workers[1], help to retain existing workers and hand the industry an important and much-needed win at a critical moment when job vacancies are high. Rested workers are more productive, fewer mistakes are made and the quality of workmanship improves.

One problem in the construction sector is the structure of contracts and work hours, which is not as neat as the 'conventional' five-day week, 9–5, but perhaps a 20 per cent reduction in total work time, or a more gradual reduction in working hours could move the industry towards more manageable work hours. Many workers are also either on agency, self-employed or on zero-hours contracts, each of which presents potential complications.

Charlie Young, a researcher, investigated the potential for a four-day week in the UK construction industry and workers he spoke to were desperate for its implementation. They also admitted that not much work gets done on a Friday anyway. Oscar Cooper, a construction worker interviewed for the report who owns a small business and works a four-day week, said:

"I can work for four days at a higher level than I could for five days. On a five-day week, on a Friday you're just watching the clock, desperate to go home, trying to chip off early. You're knackered. It's inefficient and it's dangerous."

[1.] https://6a142ff6-85bd-4a7b-bb3b-476b07b8f08d.usrfiles.com/ugd/6a142f_1d27dbad6db34288b66acf689a131da2.pdf

Given the manifold likely benefits of introducing a four-day week in construction, the 4 Day Week Campaign has proposed a series of sector-specific trials.

Other sectors that present immediate obstacles to implementation are NHS hospitals, schools and the care sector: all sectors which suffer from chronic burnout, stress and overwork alongside staff shortages.

A report backed by a public health expert, Professor John Ashton, [2]called for shorter-working-week trials to be conducted across the NHS starting with specific trusts, and, if possible, integrated care systems and primary care networks. Under these trials, NHS staff taking part would remain on the same pay. With NHS staff shortages predicted to exceed 570,000 by 2036, Professor John Ashton argued it is time to try something new to plug the gap. He said:

"Much more flexibility for NHS staff including the option of a four-day week is going to be key to ending the staff shortages we're seeing. A four-day week for NHS staff would enable people to juggle family responsibilities while maintaining their active participation in the workforce and would mean many more people are able to work longer into their 60s and beyond. With job retention levels so low, agencies are charging the NHS around 20 per cent or more extra for staff. A four-day week could dramatically improve job retention and result in this money being re-directed back towards the health service."

---

[2] https://6a142ff6-85bd-4a7b-bb3b-476b07b8f08d.usrfiles.com/ugd/6a142f_a2ebaf74380546c081ae3fcf23d9ac8f.pdf

Vacancies in the NHS already stand at 10 per cent, meaning a total of 133,000 posts need to be filled. The report, written by researcher Nic Murray, argues that overwork is a key reason for this. It found that since 2011/12, work-life balance has been cited four times more frequently than previously as a reason for leaving the NHS and is now the second most common behind retirement. The report estimates that for every three nurses to be trained by March 2024, one experienced nurse will leave because of a lack of work–life balance. Feeling unwell due to work-related stress is now a common experience among almost half of NHS staff. This represents a substantial rise over the last decade, the effects of which can snowball, affecting care quality.

This shouldn't come as a surprise given that shifts of up to twelve hours are the prevailing working pattern in British hospitals. The report found that across Europe, they are far from the norm. Twelve-hour shifts are only regularly worked by 14 per cent of nurses across Europe, most of whom are employed in three countries: Poland, Ireland and the UK. These shifts are becoming longer and longer, with less time for breaks in between, creating a toxic recipe for worker stress, and burnout and in turn risking poorer outcomes for patients. It's very clear the main reason NHS staff are quitting is a lack of work–life balance. As we've seen in other areas of the economy, there are substantial advantages to a four-day working week for both workers and employers. For the NHS it could help to improve job retention, reduce the reliance on expensive agency staff and improve the quality of care. Trials are going to be an important first step and automation could help us get there.

At Guy's and St Thomas Hospital in south London, the surgical team has utilised the strategic scheduling of patients, the use of innovative new technologies and an efficient joint-working system to significantly reduce the time needed for often complex prostate surgeries. An advanced robotic technique, adopted by the team in July 2022, for men with non-cancerous, enlarged prostates, takes an average of 40 minutes compared to the up to three hours more standard procedures would take. The team can now complete a week's worth of prostate surgeries over the course of a single day, a record for surgeries of this kind. Suitable patients were carefully selected, with their surgeries all scheduled to take place over a single day. Treatment pathways were efficiently planned, to minimise non-operative time, so that surgeons had more time to carry out the robotic-technique procedures. The consultant surgeon involved emphasised this approach *"can be applied to all surgical specialties"* and used as a *"blueprint to help tackle the rising tide of surgical waiting lists."*

Similarly, recent developments in artificial intelligence perhaps offer a viable route to a shorter working week for lots of healthcare workers in the near future. According to the world's most comprehensive trial, which took place in Sweden, the use of artificial intelligence in breast cancer screening can almost halve the workload of radiologists.[3] The trial, involving 244 women, found that screening using artificial intelligence can dramatically improve prognosis

---

[3.] https://www.theguardian.com/society/2023/aug/02/ai-use-breast-cancer-screening-study-preliminary-results

and reduce mortality by spotting breast cancer at an earlier, more treatable stage.

Turning to the care sector, there are already examples we can learn from. The Svartedalens Retirement Home in Sweden trialled moving its nursing staff, from eight hours to six a day, for the same overall pay. The centre had to hire 15 new employees for the duration of the experiment, leading to a 22 per cent hike in gross cost but found the measure led to a 10 per cent drop in sick leave and a 50 per cent improvement in the perceived health of the carers. The employees started to spend more of their work time on what analysts classified as 'social activity' with patients, such as games or outdoor walks, which is valuable for all residents, but particularly those with dementia. One of Australia's leading senior care providers, Home Instead Senior Care, switched its employees from a 48-hour work week to 32 hours over four days, with no loss in pay. The franchise owner, Myles Beaufort, said:

"It's very easy to see our revenue has actually improved ... Business has never been stronger and our team is the happiest, most productive group of people we've ever employed."

Community Integrated Care, which delivers care to more than 3,500 people across England and Scotland, announced a four-day week for 300 staff in its HR, Finance and Quality offices. It hopes to create a more supportive atmosphere for existing employees, whilst making the service attractive to new recruits. Employees have been given the option of working their usual hours but compressed over four days, taking either Monday or Friday as a non-working day. Chief People Officer, Teresa Exelby, said: *"Our colleagues have shown us how well they have adapted to a remote and hybrid working approach over the past 18 months, so we're thrilled that we're able to build on these successes as we navigate our way through the post-pandemic workplace."* They aim to further roll out the change, expanding it to their operational staff.

Finally turning to schools, the British think tank Autonomy has explored the options available for a four-day week to become a reality in schools. This ultimately comes down to a decision of whether children should stay in school for five days (with teachers rotating their days off) or also have the fifth day off. Without parents receiving an extra day off as well, it's hard to see how children across the country could move to a four-day week, highlighting the need for Government coordination around shortening the working week. In some respects, you can start to see how a four-day week in schools for teachers and children would apply upward pressure on employers to allow parents to only work four days, which could create the ripple effect needed to start spreading the four-day week far and wide. However, without proper coordination by the Government and School Board heads, it's hard to see this happening.

A report by Autonomy on the topic showed, perhaps unsurprisingly, that there is overwhelming support from teachers for introducing a four-day week to prevent teacher burnout and stop teachers from leaving the profession. In a survey of over 500 primary and secondary school teachers, included in the report, the results showed that:

- A four-day, 32-hour working week with no reduction in pay is incredibly popular among teachers with almost 75 per cent support
- Sixty-nine per cent said they would be more likely to stay in the profession if they had a four-day week
- Moving students to a four-day week, alongside teachers, is the most popular option with 45 per cent support for the school week being reduced to four days for staff and students
- Two-thirds of teachers say they've reached 'breaking point' because of their workload

In 2020, research by Ofsted found that full-time school teachers worked an average of 51 hours a week, with senior leaders putting in 57-hour weeks. This contrasts with other European countries, such as Finland, where teachers' working weeks are much shorter (34 hours). According to the UK's Health and Safety Executive, teaching staff report the highest rates of work-related stress, depression and anxiety in Britain. Chloe Tomlinson, a primary school teacher in South London, said: *"When you're refreshed and rejuvenated – those are the times when I find myself enjoying teaching most. As the term goes on, you just get worn down by the long hours. A shorter working week would make my best teaching more sustainable. You'd have happier teachers who'd be in a better place to do their jobs and keep them in the profession for longer."* Autonomy has called for a four-day week for staff and students to be seriously explored since shorter and more flexible working weeks have already become a reality for many since the Covid pandemic.

As part of a growing trend, to tackle job recruitment and retention issues, thousands of schools in rural states of the United States of America, such as Idaho, New Mexico and Oklahoma, have already shifted to a four-day week. In the UK, a shorter working week is already a reality for a handful of secondary schools that have demonstrated that reducing working hours for teachers is a real, viable possibility. Since 2019 Forest Gate Community School, Cumberland School and Waterside Academy have all moved to a shorter working week, finishing lessons at lunchtime on a Friday. Autonomy is also working with a Multi Academy Trust comprising a number of primary and secondary schools in East London to try to implement a shorter working week.

With these more challenging sectors, a recurring block is the dominance of the 9–5, five-day working week. With society largely shaped and formed around this model, it can be quite hard to see beyond it. But as the 9–5, five-day week model begins to break down and more and more people realise it is outdated and unnecessary, new opportunities will emerge, allowing us to see past and move beyond it. This shift has already begun.

5. Preparing For a Trial

"The moment your mindset shifts to a four-day week, you become naturally more efficient."

Matt Bolton, director of creative agency Mox London

The best implementations of the four-day week are well planned with thorough staff consultation beforehand. Implementation needs to be flexible and carefully calibrated. Most organisations opt for a trial first, rather than jumping straight into permanent adoption. We've found six months is the optimum duration of a trial and three the minimum. Going for a trial first gives you sufficient wriggle room to tweak and adapt things as you go, and a get-out clause if things don't go well. For reassurance, it's extremely rare an organisation tries the four-day week and goes back to five, but it's good to have the option just in case.

We've seen it rolled out best in practice when senior managers allow staff to take the lead on implementation. No one knows their job better than the person doing it, and empowering staff to be directly involved in planning tends to be the best approach. No matter what, staff must be properly consulted before implementation to tease out people's hopes and fears. This process can be initiated through a survey sent to all staff.

Pre-Trial Four-Day Week Survey Questions

Questions

1. **How would you gauge your current levels of stress *in work* on a day-to-day basis?**

   Very stressed | Stressed | Neither stressed nor not stressed | Not stressed | Not stressed at all

2. **How would you gauge your current levels of stress *outside of work* on a day-to-day basis?**

   Very stressed | Stressed | Neither stressed nor not stressed | Not stressed | Not stressed at all

3. **My job is meaningful and makes good use of my skills and talent**

   Strongly agree | Agree | Neither agree nor disagree | Disagree | Strongly disagree

4. **I am able to manage my workload in my current working hours and rarely (if ever) work overtime.**

   Strongly agree | Agree | Neither agree nor disagree | Disagree | Strongly disagree

5. **If you answered 'Disagree' or 'Strongly Disagree' to the above question, please provide an estimation of the average number of hours of overtime you complete on a weekly basis.**

6.   How satisfied are you with the amount of free time you have outside of work?

Very satisfied | Satisfied | Neither satisfied nor dissatisfied | Dissatisfied | Very dissatisfied

7.   My current working hours have made it easier for me to pursue personal interests and hobbies as well as complete 'life admin' (cleaning, washing, cooking etc.).

Strongly agree | Agree | Neither agree nor disagree | Disagree | Strongly disagree

8.   My current working hours have made it easier for me to manage my personal responsibilities, such as childcare and other caring roles.

Strongly agree | Agree | Neither agree nor disagree | Disagree | Strongly disagree

9.   On a scale on 1 to 5, how highly do you value the flexibility afforded by home working?

1 not at all | 5 very much

10.   The working culture within the company provides personal autonomy within my role.

Strongly agree | Agree | Neither agree nor disagree | Disagree | Strongly disagree

11.   The division of labour within the team is efficient and effective.

Strongly agree | Agree | Neither agree nor disagree | Disagree | Strongly disagree

12.   Please use this space if you would like to elaborate on your answer above

13.   Being totally honest, on average how many hours in your current working day do you consider productive (done in a fully motivated manner)?

14.   As an organisation, we collaborate well on a day-to-day basis to deliver our expected workload.

Strongly agree | Agree | Neither agree nor disagree | Disagree | Strongly disagree

15.   Please use this space if you would like to elaborate on your answer above.

16.   Within my team/department, we collaborate well on a day-to-day basis to deliver our expected workload.

Strongly agree | Agree | Neither agree nor disagree | Disagree | Strongly disagree

17.   Please use this space if you would like to elaborate on your answer above.

18.   I am confident I can successfully adapt my work processes to suit a four-day week.

Strongly agree | Agree | Neither agree nor disagree | Disagree | Strongly disagree

19.   How confident are you that a four-day week is a sustainable way of working for [insert name of organisation]?

Very confident | Somewhat confident | Neither confident nor not confident | Somewhat not confident | Not confident at all

Beyond sending round a survey, an all-staff meeting can be organised to discuss plans. There may also be smaller meetings involving line managers, as well as department or team meetings. Many organisations have emphasised the positivity and team cohesion generated by bringing their team together this way.

The optimum amount of time to spend preparing for a trial is usually three months. This depends on the size of your organisation as in larger organisations there will be more people to consult. But once board approval is in place, three months is usually plenty of time to prepare.

A worry we hear all the time from staff is that of being able to complete their work in four days rather than five. Abigail Morris, accounts director at Target Publishing, a media publication operating on a four-day week, says: *"I think the preconception is that you can't get everything done, that you won't have enough time to get your workload done."* However, the opposite seems to happen and this fear almost always disappears once the four-day week has been implemented. It's important to have these conversations as a team beforehand and make sure steps can be put in place to mitigate these concerns. Steps such as tweaking work patterns, working smarter and finding ways to improve business performance, which you'll hear more about in the next chapter.

It's worth noting that at this point in the process, there can be a real danger of overthinking things. We've seen a handful of companies overthink every single possible eventuality and get totally hamstrung when the whole point of doing a trial is to see what happens and make improvements along the way. You should never go into a trial expecting everything to work smoothly straight away, but after a month or two, once people have got into the groove of it, most problems tend to fade away.

Alison Dunn, chief executive of Citizen's Advice Gateshead, recalled her fear at this stage:

"One of the things that was really on my mind as the leader of this organisation was all the terrible things that I was absolutely convinced were going to go wrong. I literally wrote them down – a long list of everything that could possibly

have happened and what I was going to do when each of those things happened. In reality, not one of them happened."

Her advice: *"You just have to take a leap of faith. Once you have decided you're going, just go."*

Matt Bolton, director of a creative agency called Mox London which took part in the UK pilot, offers some further words of advice: *"The moment your mindset shifts to a four-day week, you become naturally more efficient."* He's right and as someone who has worked a four-day week for the last five years, I can back that up. When I write my to-do list for the week I schedule my work into four days rather than five and make sure the work that needs to be done, gets done. This is exactly the same as I would have done over five days previously but I'm now much more time efficient. Sometimes that can involve a slightly busier week, or a busier Thursday afternoon racing to finish everything for the reward of Friday off – but that often feels good and you soon realise how much time is wasted working across five days.

Matt is a big advocate of the four-day week and says it has been a major positive for his organisation and him personally: *"On a personal level, having an extra day off every week has been huge. It allows me to spend more time with my family and my son. Also, from a work perspective, it surprised me how much more focused I am."*

As well as being more focused, you become more motivated working across four days. The dread that can arrive on Monday morning when faced with the reality of working for the next five days in a row dissipates under a four-day week and often leads to higher performance at work. This is because when workers enjoy their work more, they tend to perform better.

More motivation = better performance + productivity.

You should also consider this: the average employee is only productive for two hours and 53 minutes a day anyway, according to one study[1]. This equates to only 15 productive hours a week meaning there is a lot of wasted time working across five days. This wasted time becomes less over four days and as a result our brains become clearer and more focused on the work that needs to get done. This is a problem that has only been exacerbated in recent times since there are now the distractions of smartphones and social media all around us, all of the time. We'll discuss some strategies for dealing with this in the next chapter.

Preparing for the Four-day Week in a Housing Association

A housing association with approximately 250 employees has many functions: building maintenance, running a community youth service, operating several community centres and keeping the neighbourhood tidy.

The association (which wished to remain anonymous) is run as a mutual, guided by a democratic body of employees and tenants. It is responsible for electing a board, whose CEO compares the organisation to a fan-owned football club: *"It's power-sharing."* In line

[1] https://www.oak.com/blog/employee-productivity-statistics/

with these governance principles, the organisation was firm about the fact that any four-day week policy would have to be shaped in a democratic fashion while being flexible enough to include all staff. This meant that the differing daily challenges of office teams, community-facing teams, and trades teams all had to be considered.

To incorporate this diversity, the organisation opted for a decentralised four-day week, with different working patterns in different departments. The CEO believed that staff with experience on the ground were best equipped to make key decisions. Each department was therefore supported in designing its own four-day week model.

"We took the decision that everyone knows their own job better than anyone else," said the CEO. In the buildup to the pilot, all staff members took part in pre-trial workshops with their teams, envisioning how the four-day workweek might change their lives and debating the best implementation model to fit the nature of their work. Each team then produced a two-minute video explaining their chosen four-day week model. These videos were then shared across the organisation.

The staff we interviewed about the preparation process described a need to find a sweet spot between coverage requirements and staff preferences. Some teams opted to use a rolling four-day week rota system, in which staff book their days off at the start of each month. This allowed staff to fit work around their personal priorities on a shifting basis. Reflecting on the pilot preparation period, staff always praised the pilot as a catalyst for innovation around work processes. The CEO repeatedly described the pilot process as 'refreshing':

"The conversations people were having, they would not have had if not for the shared incentive of making this work ... It has been like flicking on a switch for some folks."

We heard a lot of stories about the time-saving ideas generated in the preparatory workshops. The trades staff reduced their travel time to and from the building supplier by knowing which materials are needed before they leave and organising their van more efficiently.

They also now feel comfortable going home early when there is less to do. Office teams are automating certain processes and redesigning others to involve fewer personnel. Community-facing teams have taken lessons from remote working, realising some smaller issues can be dealt with adequately over the phone.

The staff and CEO were all clearly proud of the collective approach taken to the pilot preparations, describing it as a positive experience. Staff knowledge and involvement were seen as key to making the four-day week a sincere and realistic policy, rather than an empty gesture.

The CEO said: *"What we don't want is this underground of people who are notionally working a four-day week but secretly working at the weekend to catch up."*

...

A slightly more unusual approach in preparation for a trial was taken by skincare cosmetics company, 5 Squirrels, based in Brighton. Rather than implementing the four-day week on an agreed date, they gradually introduced it over a period of four weeks. In week nine of their 12-week preparation, staff left at 3pm on a Friday. In week 10, staff left at 1pm, Week 11 – 11am and by week 12 they were more than ready to skip Friday altogether.

In many respects, this is not dissimilar to many organisations that have already introduced nine-day fortnights. The nine-day fortnight is effectively 50 per cent of the way to a four-day week so definitely another option to consider for organisations that don't feel ready to go the full hurdle, which could help pave the way for eventually achieving a true four-day week.

Gary Conroy, CEO of 5 Squirrels, is a big advocate of the four-day week and has taken part in two four-day-week rollout programmes as an ambassador. His organisation took part in the 61-company major UK pilot and the trial at 5 Squirrels was so successful that Gary's was one of the 18 companies that decided to make the move permanent as soon as the trial ended. Speaking about how they did it, he said:

> *"The world of work is changing and we wanted to place the emphasis on productivity, not hours worked. We're trying to run a profitable, productive company and we believe that one of the ways of doing that is by having higher employee engagement and happier members of staff who are not burnt out the whole time and have a good quality of life outside work. We can get a lot more done in less time, meaning that we are then free to have more time off."*

Gary's dedication to the preparation period was stronger than most and he said they introduced 'deep work' time (which we'll hear more about in Chapter Six) to help with productivity: dedicated two-hour working periods without emails or messages to distract staff. They also cut meetings back to a bare minimum, and those scheduled could only be during certain time periods for a maximum of 30 minutes.

Week 1 - 4 (12 weeks pre-pilot)

- Every task recorded in outlook diaries
  - Casual chats
  - Phone calls
  - Breaks
- Amnesty for honesty
- No judgement
- KPI's to record tasks and type achieved per week

Week 4 - 8 (8 weeks pre-pilot)

- Clustering tasks
  - Each similar group of tasks placed into time blocks
  - Goals set for number of tasks completed per time block
  - Email, Teams etc classed as a cluster
- Meetings reduced to 30 mins
- Regular recurring meetings reduced to reports
- All meetings to be conducted between 9-10 am, 12-2pm or 4-5pm.
- Introduction of deep work time at all other times
- Stop answering landline and responding to messages via email
- Personal phone amnesty – off or "in the box"
- Introduce Focus Matrix – Prioritize, Deprioritize etc

Week 8 -12 (4 weeks pre-pilot)

- Plan all meetings and task clusters Mon-Thurs only, use Friday as safety net
- No meetings on Fridays
- Regular recurring meetings reduced to reports
- Last shipments to customers on Thursdays
- Only respond to urgent emails or call son Fridays
- Bring task forward from following week if safety net not required
- Week 9 – leave at 3pm
- Week 10 – leave at 1pm
- Week 11 – leave at 11 am

Preparation is crucial but at the same time make sure not to overthink things. No business owner should implement the four-day week overnight, but neither should you tear your hair out worrying about all the possible things that could go wrong. It's a balance.

If you need extra support, the 4-Day Week Campaign and Autonomy run a regular eight-week rollout programme with online workshops designed to take you through the process. Autonomy and a number of other organisations and individuals also offer bespoke consultancy support for organisations that may need extra help.

Finally, don't forget the point of a trial is to test and tweak things as you go. Even if you think you've managed to prepare for every single possible eventuality, there's always a leap of faith involved. This is the most nerve-wracking part of the process, but stay clear and focused on your intentions and remember, you are on the right side of history.

6. Improving Business Performance: Working Smarter, Not Harder

"The four-day work week is achieved not by placing the burden on individuals to become faster and more productive, but through getting better at prioritising and de-prioritising."

Banks Benitez, CEO of Uncharted

A four-day week is eminently possible for every business in the long term, yet it is understandable that some companies remain hesitant. Some may feel it impossible for employees to get the same amount of work done in four days as five, while others could feel employees may be pushed even harder to cram five days' worth of work into four. The truth is that, if done right, both of these concerns prove unfounded.

Moving to a four-day week is about working smarter, not harder, assessing dominant paradigms around work and changing our mindsets to adopt a greater level of organisation and planning. It's a change which organisations should embrace – as Claire Daniels, CEO of Trio Media, a marketing agency which took part in the big UK pilot, did:

"The four-day week is a great opportunity to shine a spotlight on your business and processes and see how you can improve them. We made so many efficiency gains that we would have probably never considered without the move to a four-day week."

Crucially, there are a number of practical steps you can take to improve business performance and more effectively attune your organisation to a four-day working pattern.

Hustle Culture

Much of the problem lies in our current perception of work; society has embraced an unhealthy mindset around it and much of the way we work is inefficient. Society's attitude to work has been captured by hustle culture. Hustle culture is a very loose and colloquial term, but it is generally defined as a mindset that obsesses over the quantity of work we do – that more equals better. Put simply, people think working harder and longer is a badge of honour and that it will produce a greater likelihood of career success. This logic defines many people's attitudes to work.

This manifests itself in other areas of our working lives. Not only do people strive to be seen to be working all the time, even if this leads to no tangible or effective output, but they also feel the need to be constantly available, either to co-workers or clients. The popularity and widespread adoption of hustle culture largely stems from anecdotes about high-profile entrepreneurs from the mid-2000s, many of which emphasised the nature of working every waking hour in pursuit of your goals.[1] People have come to equate these stories with a recipe for success, so much so that the insurance company Aviva remarked that hustle culture has *"defined our collective working lives for decades.*[2]

This has resulted in highly unhealthy working environments where employees feel stressed, overwhelmed and, ultimately, burnt out. In 2019, the WHO classified burnout as an occupation phenomenon. A Microsoft survey found that over 50% of employees in 11 different countries were suffering from burnout.[3] This is even more pronounced in the UK, where we work some of the longest full-time hours in the world. According to a study commissioned by LumApps, a leading employee experience platform: *"88% of UK employees have experienced at least some level of burnout over the last two years, with one-third claiming to suffer from physical and mental exhaustion frequently due to pressures within the workplace."*[4]

These statistics are concerning because burnout has been linked to a high proportion of resignations and, even more worryingly, a number of serious physical and mental

---

[1] https://www.bbc.com/worklife/article/20230417-hustle-culture-is-this-the-end-of-rise-and-grind

[2] https://www.aviva.co.uk/business/business-perspectives/featured-articles-hub/signs-of-quiet-quitting/

[3] https://www.forbes.com/sites/edwardsegal/2022/10/15/surveys-show-burnout-is-an-international-crisis/

[4] https://employernews.co.uk/news/88-of-uk-workforce-have-experienced-burnout-in-the-past-two-years-reveals-research-by-lumapps/

illnesses.[5] There has been some pushback against hustle culture, as people are increasingly realising the harm it has on both physical and mental well-being. Yet, even as people become aware of this, they still feel trapped in the culture by the logic of competition in the workplace. People then internalise this culture by telling themselves, *'If I don't work my socks off, someone else will and they'll take my place, so I'll just have to suck it up.'*

Hustle culture is not only damaging in the results it produces but also because of how ingrained it is within our cultural attitude. It breeds a kind of unfounded resistance to the four-day week. When we equate long working hours and greater physical and mental exertion with success, naturally reducing the working week by a whole day is baulked at for a business wanting to remain competitive: working fewer hours will mean less work is completed, leading to lower revenues and slower growth – making the company less competitive, or so hustle-culture logic dictates. This fuels the idea that the four-day week is not possible because we are all already working at full capacity. Under this reasoning, to reduce working time by a full eight-hour day would either be impossible or force us to exert ourselves further in a smaller time frame, to compensate.

---

[5] https://www.theguardian.com/money/2021/nov/01/the-great-resignation-almost-one-in-four-workers-planning-job-change; Salvagioni, Denise Albieri Jodas et al. "Physical, psychological and occupational consequences of job burnout: A systematic review of prospective studies." *Plos One*, Volume 12 (October 2017) doi:10.1371/journal.pone.0185781 https://www.ncbi.nlm.nih.gov/pmc/articles/PMC5627926/

Dispelling the Myth: Working Smarter Not Harder

This is in fact, not what the data tells us. As we have seen in previous chapters, a four-day week actually makes employees more productive and innovative. To put it simply: rested workers are better workers. We can very easily move to a four-day week that produces comparable and even improved results – not by working harder, but smarter. We don't have to work harder in less time to produce the same outcome. We just have to rethink and reorganise the inefficient and outdated parts of our working practices, like the five-day workweek. This means adopting a new mindset and replacing the idea that more is the key to success, with realising that less is sometimes more. This means restructuring and redefining the way we work to become more results-oriented and make better decisions. The key is, in fact, to redesign the way we work for more efficient time management and workflow.

Banks Benitez and Uncharted

One entrepreneur who understands this and has whole-heartedly embraced new ways of working to implement a successful four-day week is the American CEO of Uncharted, Banks Benitez. Uncharted, a Denver-based social invest-ment accelerator, moved permanently to a four-day week in September 2020, following a trial beginning in April that year. Both the quantity and quality of employee performance did not change, as measured against Key Performance Indicators

(KPIs) taken before the trial start date. Work–life balance improved and employee stress decreased. This became apparent soon into the trial period. The company's recruitment and retention capabilities also increased. But how was the company able to move to a four-day week while maintaining productivity?

There were three key factors involved. The first of these was a move to output-focused working. This started from the fundamental understanding that the number of hours worked does not translate into the quality of the work performed. Instead, Uncharted began to focus more heavily on what drove real results for the company and tailored its operations to centre on them. The mantra for this shift was, that time invested matters less than results produced. *"The four-day workweek is achieved not by placing the burden on individuals to become faster and more productive, but through getting better at prioritising and de-prioritising,"* says Benitez.

This insight was built on the infamous Pareto principle, named after the 19th-century Italian economist Vilfredo Pareto and refined by the academic and management consultant Joseph M Juran, which states that 80 per cent of all results come from just 20 per cent of the work. The Pareto principle has applications in all walks of life, but holds particularly true in business and productivity practices. Microsoft, for example, found that *"80 per cent of the errors in Windows and Office are caused by just 20 per cent of the entire pool of bugs."*[6] The logic follows that if they focus their efforts on fixing just 20 per cent of bugs, they

---

[6] https://www.crn.com/news/security/18821726/microsofts-ceo-80-20-rule-applies-to-bugs-not-just-features.htm

will actually prevent 80 per cent of errors. This is much less time-consuming and much more effective than fixing every single bug, one at a time.

By shifting the focus to what actually produces results, and reorienting business practice around it, you begin to operate more efficiently.[7] If we spend our working time focusing on what generates the best results, we are making the most productive use of our time. This allows the business to develop at a more streamlined rate. When time is managed more efficiently, growth is boosted as the work carried out is always productive.

It also creates a reduction in stress and burnout, identified at the beginning of this chapter as detrimental to both health and work-related performance. If we are able to streamline working patterns and focus them more clearly, employees don't suffer from increasing demands being placed upon them that ultimately lead to burnout. This in turn decreases staff turnover, which saves heaps of time onboarding and training new staff. Equally, it gives employees greater space and clarity to think while at work, increasing the frequency of lightbulb ideas that can grow the business and make it even more successful.

Giving employees a clearer focus will also help improve decision-making. When workers know what is actually important and have been given the mandate to prioritise it, they are more likely to make accurate decisions which lead to improvements. As Greg McKeown, author and CEO of an eponymous leadership and design agency in California, has

---

[7] "Pareto Principles: Examples of the 80/20 rule for Business Success," *Santander*, 2nd March 2023 https://www.becas-santander.com/en/blog/pareto-principle-examples.html

observed, using data from over one hundred teams, *"when there is a high level of clarity ... people thrive."*[8]

The shift to output-focused working ensures resources are deployed in the most effective manner possible, as resources will be more effectively spent on what produces the best outcomes, reducing waste and optimising performance. Overall, it promotes better dialogue between senior managers and workers on what work the company should be doing. In this manner, leaders are held more accountable by staff, creating greater democratisation in the workplace, with everyone feeling they are contributing significantly to the business's success.

While this method helps us highlight what work is essential, this does not mean the other 80 per cent of tasks should be discarded. It is only to say that paying greater attention to the minority of work that produces the majority of important results will allow you to work more effectively. This is why Juran referred to the 20/80 Pareto distribution as *"the vital few and the useful many."*

We should focus on quality over quantity and design the way we work around this. Indeed, it seems strange that the phrase 'quality over quantity' has been a widely regarded part of our collective general wisdom for many years. Why haven't we applied it to work? Uncharted did, and it was one of the main reasons they were able to transition smoothly to a four-day week.

The next thing Uncharted did was to rethink the decision-making process and place more weight on making

---

8. Greg McKeown, *Essentialism: The Disciplined Pursuit of Less* (London: Virgin Books, 2014) 121

future-proof decisions. Decision-making is important and Benitez recognises this, citing making effective decisions as another key ingredient for successfully implementing a four-day week. Poor decision-making can negatively affect productivity, revenue, reputation and staff motivation. According to Benitez, making better decisions is the best substitute for working longer.

We have already seen how moving to output-focused working can help us make better decisions. It tells us where to focus the majority of our efforts, where to deploy our limited resources and how to organise our work in order to get the best results. However, good decision-making doesn't stop once you have identified these things. It's a constantly evolving process that can keep your organisation on track and ensure it remains streamlined and agile. The key to success is to design decision-making processes that lead to better outcomes.

One good decision now can prevent a hundred downstream decisions arising from a poor alternative.[9] Decisions need to be made to continually maintain optimal performance and eliminate needless problems that sap time and energy, creating drags on productivity. Decisions made either too hastily, in an emotional state, or focusing on short-term success, without adequate data, are just some examples that could potentially lead to unnecessary work down the road. Priority should be given to ensuring the correct decisions are taken so that workers' energy is continually focused on the drivers of results, not preventable distractions.

[9.] Greg McKeown, *Essentialism: The Disciplined Pursuit of Less* (London: Virgin Books, 2014) 119-131

Alongside the move to output-focused working and redesigning the decision-making process, Benitez rethought his company's approach to client relations. Many client-facing businesses are aware of the prevalence of what might be called the 'customer is always right' mentality and will often fall into the trap of working harder and longer to deliver. Their view is that if the client wants something done, they are obligated to do it, even if that means working every waking hour available. It is completely understandable that any business wants to offer the best service possible. But this can be done without relenting to hustle culture, and easily within the confines of the four-day week.

Uncharted was able to provide the same high level of service by working smarter, not harder. Just as it conducted a Pareto inventory to identify what really drove results in the business, it also conducted a similar, client-based inventory, identifying factors commonly leading to the best client outcomes, prioritising these to drive its service going forward. It identified successful strategies and areas where time was wasted, along with opportunities for other efficiencies and improvements. This client audit allowed it to deliver a comparable and, in some cases, better service in a smaller time frame. Again, by focusing on the drivers of results, it was able to provide the same level of service in four days, simply by working smarter.

In order to ensure the new working pattern could be implemented properly, Benitez was careful to set positive boundaries and communicate them effectively, being open and honest with clients. Good communication from the outset of a client relationship is always essential, but even more so when your business operates a four-day week. One of the strengths of Uncharted's approach was that it was proactive rather than reactive. In order to build positive working relationships, it listed non-negotiables with clients upfront and clearly delineated working hours, ensuring the available time was used for client communications. Most importantly, it also explained that its aim in moving to a four-day week was to work smarter and more efficiently to deliver, at the very least, the same level of service.

No doubt many clients will welcome the positives from working with a business that seeks to improve staff wellbeing and business performance by adopting a four-day week. But what about clients who breach the boundaries set by four-day week employers, expecting five days of work to feel they are truly getting value for money? This is rare in our experience, but clients who repeatedly try to breach any non-negotiables agreed upon at the outset may prove difficult to work with. If problems arise once a partnership or working dynamic has been formed, Benitez recommends releasing clients who prove to be highly problematic. In summary, we've always found a proactive communication strategy with clients is the best approach. Be confident and clear in communicating what you intend to achieve by moving to a four-day week and emphasise that the quality of work will not be affected. Most clients will be fine with this, and many will welcome this dynamic new approach.

Uncharted is a perfect example of how a company can move to a four-day week by working smarter, not harder. The company was able to maintain employee performance, improve work-life balance, decrease stress levels and see benefits to staff recruitment and retention, simply by reorganising and rethinking how the company operated. A four-day week that maintains productivity and, in some cases, improves it, is absolutely possible if implemented correctly. Simple measures such as focusing on what produces results, making good decisions and clearly communicating with clients allowed Uncharted to move to a four-day week with no drop in performance. The key to implementation is tweaking business practices to become more efficient by focusing on the drivers of real results and making good decisions, reorienting business practices around them and communicating this effectively with clients.

Preparing in this way will make the transition to a four-day week smoother.

Practical Steps: How to Work Smarter, not Harder

We have already discussed some principles of the four-day week, like working smarter, not harder and what this might look like in practice. But how can we go about implementing them and how might they be combined with practical, productivity-maximising tools, to tweak business performance and get your organisation four-day week ready?

1. Staff Consultation and Inventory

As we have seen, consulting staff should be the first thing you do when considering moving to a four-day week. Discuss why the company wants to do this and how it could be implemented. The best way is to conduct an inventory with staff which will help establish how you can work more efficiently:

- As an organisation, identify the drivers of real results and build your four-day week around them. Start with a Pareto inventory – which 20 per cent of the work is essential to the results that truly matter – and work from there
- Similarly, identify what could be unnecessary and eliminate it. Close-up analysis of current work routines shows that on average 20 per cent of tasks are 'clutter tasks,' unproductive work that adds no value to the business. These tasks can be cut, with no negative effect on the business
- Change job descriptions to focus on outcomes: remove unnecessary tasks which take up lots of time, but do not actually contribute towards the organisational outcome an employee has been hired to achieve; this may not be necessary but is worth considering

2. Prioritise Tasks

Once an inventory has been conducted, prioritise the work you have decided to keep, to bring greater clarity and streamline the decision-making process. Prioritising tasks allows you to accomplish them more effectively

- Experiment with a Focus Matrix to help prioritise your workload

- Focus on the most important tasks first and defer those less important
- Assess employees' skills and assign tasks to the most suited
- Group similar tasks together to achieve them more quickly

3. Introduce Focused Time

Once work has been prioritised, introduce focused time to complete it more efficiently and productively. This is especially important nowadays with the rise of social media on the smartphones in our pockets, where we're always just one click away from being distracted.

	Low Value	High Value
High Effort		
Low Effort		

Figure 1: Focus Matrix – The focus matrix was invented by Dwight D Eisenhower to help him manage and win his 1952 presidential campaign. It helps prioritise workloads, allowing you to sort tasks by urgency and importance.

- Designate points at the beginning and end of the day to attend meetings and compose emails (e.g. 9.10am for meetings and 4–5pm for emails)
- Use the rest of the day to have large chunks of focused 'work' time
- Consider placing your personal mobile phone away from your desk, to avoid distractions and temptations during focused time

One company taking part in the UK pilot went even further and introduced a 'traffic light' system to prevent unnecessary distractions. Lights were installed on colleagues' desks allowing them to set it to 'green' if they were happy to talk, 'amber' if they were busy but available to speak and 'red' if they absolutely did not want to be interrupted.

4. Revise Meetings

'Let's set up a meeting to discuss the meeting that we just met about before we meet next time.'
Seably, a Four-Day Week Maritime Training Company based in Sweden

Meetings are a source of wasted time in most organisations. 'Having a meeting, about a meeting, about a meeting' is common in British workplaces and addressing this can be an easy way to gain back time. A survey of 31,000 Microsoft employees found that inefficient meetings are the greatest distraction in the workplace, followed closely by having too many meetings, both of which harm productivity.[10]

- Cut out unnecessary meetings
- Halve the length of the remaining meetings
- Ensure everyone attending genuinely needs to be there
- This process can be aided by ensuring all work meetings are preceded by the creation of an agenda shared at least an hour before the meeting

5. Experiment With New Software and Technology

Experimenting with new types of software can help streamline work communications, saving time in the process. This is perhaps geared more towards companies with the financial resources to do so, but investing in new technology can also help in other areas of the business and improve subsequent performance.

- Try using new communication software, such as Slack, that allows multiple employees to communicate with each other at the same time, ensuring decisions are made more quickly
- Task management software, such as Asana, allows managers to organise their workload and delegate tasks clearly to employees more effectively

---

- Artificial intelligence, including platforms like ChatGPT, should also be able to help find efficiencies

Once you have identified how your organisation can save time and work smarter, start putting this into practice as you prepare for your trial.

7. Running a Trial and Measuring Success

"Our metrics and people surveys show that this has not had a negative impact on employees or customer service. In fact, it has been the opposite, with happier, more efficient, and more productive people who are even more driven to help us change banking for the better. We believe most organisations can move to a four-day week and we hope Atom's experience will encourage more businesses to make the shift permanently."

Anne-Marie Lister, Chief People Officer at Atom Bank

In the days prior to starting a trial, there is usually a lot of excitement amongst staff. At this point, you are hopefully well-prepared and ready to take the leap of faith together as an organisation. Again, remember to anticipate and expect some problems along the way, but know that these can be fixed as the trial progresses. During the trial period, nothing dramatic really needs to happen. Your organisation should continue trying to achieve what it usually sets out to, just with one day less but all the extra focus, commitment and efficiency that comes with the four-day week.

Many four-day week companies like to have check-ins with staff throughout the trial period. These could take place every week, to begin with, then less frequently towards the end. Having a halfway point check-in is certainly a good idea.

Where staff are rotating days off instead of all having the same fixed one a sufficient and effective handover process is key. Ensuring there is time to check this is working in the first couple of weeks has been crucial for some organisations we have helped.

Staff surveys are the best way to find out what impact the move has had, if any, on staff wellbeing. The best approach here is to take a baseline survey before the trial begins, another in the middle and again at the end. This will very clearly show the impact the move has had on issues such as burnout, stress, overwork, job satisfaction and more.

When measuring success for your company or organisation, you want to be even more clear about what you are measuring. Measures of productivity will vary from business to business. For some, it will be a pure revenue metric, for others the number of product units sold, the number of customers won or managed, or any other measurable success. The key is to ensure that, whichever metric is used, a baseline is set before embarking on a four-day week. For many companies, success simply means profits: have profits been maintained or improved over the trial period? But for other organisations, profits won't be that relevant and success could be measured by something else entirely. For example, an NGO we worked with defined success with the number of successful campaigns they ran on a monthly/yearly basis. This was measured by parameters they had in place to check if a campaign was reaching its targets and then ultimately whether the campaign was successful in achieving its demands.

As set out in Chapter Three, for many organisations an increase in wellbeing is enough in itself and any other benefits are seen as a bonus. Either way, it's important you are very clear on what you hope to achieve and how you are going to measure the impact. Most companies will already measure various KPIs to assess performance so it's simply a case of seeing how they have changed after the trial begins. But if there's something you would like to measure that you are not already measuring, it's important you identify it and figure out exactly how to measure success in this area. Bringing in expert research consultancy could be useful here. In the resources section at the end of the book, I've listed a group of academics and researchers who might be able to help you.

Setting clear parameters for measuring success is also really important if you want to persuade the board to permanently adopt a four-day week. If the data shows the company is performing better and staff are happier, it will be hard for them to refuse. As Gary Conroy, CEO of 5 Squirrels, says:

> *"Our productivity is up, our profitability is up, our sales are up, our output is up. So why would you go back to dragging it out into another day? It's really counterintuitive."*

For Atom Bank, the UK's largest four-day week employer with over 500 employees and one of the biggest digital challenger banks, the impact on customers was just as important as the impact on staff. It decided the best way to measure the customer impact was through its Trustpilot score – the main UK platform for customer reviews. To measure customer goodwill, it used metrics like App Store ratings, customer complaints and customer feedback sentiment. Atom Bank is nearly three years into adopting the four-day week now, but data it released after 10 months of trialling it[1] showed that its Trustpilot score had risen from 4.54 (out of 5) to 4.82 and its customer goodwill score from 83.1 per cent to 85.8 per cent. Staff surveys showed that 91 per cent of staff were able to get everything done within four days and 92 per cent felt encouraged to find efficiencies. Productivity had also increased across the vast majority of departmental metrics.

Speaking at the time, Anne-Marie Lister, Chief People Officer at Atom Bank, said:

"Over nine months on from introducing our new four-day working week, it's clear that it has been a huge success for our business and our people. We are extremely proud of how our employees have adapted and the benefit it has brought to many. Our metrics and people surveys show that this has not had a negative impact on employees or customer service. In fact, it has been the opposite, with happier, more efficient, and more productive people who are even more driven to help us change banking for the better.

[1.] https://www.atombank.co.uk/blog/four-day-week-10-months-on/

"Moving to a four-day week has meant a fundamental shift in our operating model and working practice. We did not expect that it would be easy and knew there would be challenges along the way. That's why we have adopted the mindset that we need to work hard to overcome these difficulties in order to make the shift work. Our business and people have benefited from this persistence, which is certainly required if you are to challenge traditional ways of working that have been in place for almost 100 years.

"We firmly believe the four-day week is the future of working life and it is encouraging to now see the range of businesses across the UK embracing the four-day week trials. We are a progressive bank and a progressive employer, and our experience in planning for and moving to a four-day week has shown that it is possible for businesses to do this and bring huge benefits to their people. We believe most organisations can move to a four-day week and we hope Atom's experience will encourage more businesses to make the shift permanently."

In 2015, CMG Technologies, a leading metal injection moulding producer based in Suffolk, decided to move to a four-day week. Rachel Garrett, managing director, said this decision was motivated by a desire to improve staff wellbeing and job retention as well as to attract talented workers. CMG is a highly specialised company and recruiting and training new staff can be a challenge.

Management approached staff to propose the new working model and asked each team to discuss how to reconfigure shift patterns to reduce hours and ensure cover was always there when needed. Directors then reviewed these proposals to assess whether they were reasonable, before implementing the new shifts. They now have shift patterns where some employees work Monday to Thursday, some Tuesday to Friday, and others work weekend shifts. This ensures someone is always on the shop floor and use of the machinery is maximised.

Because people chose to make their working-time reductions in different ways – some opted for shorter hours across 5 days – one challenge was to work out how to assign holidays. To do this, CMG changed its system to one where holidays were counted in hours rather than days. It calculated people's hours of holiday based on the hours in each person's average working day, multiplying that by the amount of days they were previously assigned.

A key challenge was ensuring that output could be maintained despite the loss of labour. It did this by investing in robotics as well as scrutinising existing processes to identify labour-intensive parts and see how those aspects could be optimised. It now has less scrap and a more efficient process. These technological improvements involved small up-front costs, which have been more than paid for by a consistent uplift in profits, turnover and productivity since introducing the four-day week. This is in part attributable to employee retention being very high, so it is not constantly spending time and money on recruitment and training. The better work–life balance also means sick leave is at an all-time low.

Rachel says that since making the change, employees are much more likely to 'give their all' to the job because they feel cared for by their employer, and 'better in themselves.' Having the extra time to do life admin, book appointments and recuperate means they return to work refreshed and motivated.

Another nice thing we've seen a few organisations do during a trial is to get staff to share pictures with the rest of the team, highlighting what they are getting up to on their extra day off. This can be a nice way for everyone to see how people are benefiting and for managers to get some recognition for their decisions. Everyone is different so people will use their time off differently but some of the most popular ways to use this extra time can include: life admin, volunteering, hobbies, holidays, more time with family and resting.

Four-day Week Trial at Citizen's Advice, Gateshead

Victoria, 38, has been a case worker at the charity Citizen's Advice (Gateshead) for five years. Victoria says having 20 per cent of her hours cut while remaining on full pay has sharpened her focus during working hours and eased the stress of childcare. With two children, one just starting school and an elder child who is disabled, the new working arrangement allows Victoria to be a constant in her children's lives, and do the school run each day. She said:

"Our eldest son has complex needs and routine means everything to him. Knowing that the children have quality time and reassurance of routine with me, means I have had a weight lifted and I can be really focused on work. It is working so well, and I am feeling really productive, consistently hitting my weekly target."

Paul Oliver, 49, chief operating officer at Citizens Advice, Gateshead, said the charity was keen on the idea of a four-day week as a way of improving job recruitment and retention:

"We wanted a way of delivering our services that ensured our clients were getting the best level of support from well-rested and more productive staff and the four-day week was a game changer for us in that respect. We're really pleased with the results so far. In the months following the launch of the trial, our sickness levels went down and staff retention levels went up, bucking the trend shown by other similar organisations recently.

"It feels like it's really making a difference in so many crucial ways. Staff are getting more work done in less time and overall working more efficiently and effectively. Most of our services are seeing more clients than they were before the trial."

Louise, 50, is a consumer advisor at the charity who says the four-day week pilot allows her to be a more supportive partner and mum. Having been employed by the charity for nearly four years, Louise works in the hectic legal rights department, supporting people with issues such as faulty goods and services, scam calls, doorstep callers and traders knocking on doors.

Louise has chosen to take Thursdays off. She says it has had a massive impact on her household:

"Personally, the four-day week means I can have my own time and get my jobs done. I go to Scotland [to visit her new partner] every other weekend, and my daughter is having an operation soon, so fitting her appointments in on a Thursday means I can go with her. This means I feel more relaxed and pass that benefit back to the charity.

"Workwise we are in a good position as we have quite a big team, around 30 of us, and it hasn't affected our team performance or achievements negatively at all. In fact, all of our targets are being hit and each team member is currently helping 30–35 people on calls each day as an experienced advisor. Our clients are benefiting from an even higher quality service as we are all more refreshed. It is an intense role and you get tired by the end of the week, so that extra day break allows you to be your best at all times."

** Some surnames have been redacted for confidentiality

• • •

Once the trial is over, you will need to make an assessment. To do this, you should look at all the evidence you have collected about the impact on staff and your organisation. If the trial has been a success, you may want to seek board approval to make the move permanent (see Chapter Four for advice on making contractual changes).

Once a decision has been made to permanently continue with the four-day week, don't forget to seek accreditation through the 4 Day Week Campaign (see resources at the end) so you can become an official four-day week employer and share your story with the world.

If you've reached this stage of the process and are about to begin a trial, good luck to you! We hope you can take courage from the stories of those who have gone before.

8. Organising For a Four-Day Week in the Workplace

The successful campaign that won us the weekend and the 40-hour working week in the 1930s and 1940s was victorious because workers made their voices heard, with the support of their trade unions. We're long overdue another major reduction in working time but can't rely on all bosses to make that change unless there is pressure from below. Building on the history of the movement for shorter working time, I'm going to set out what you, as a worker, could do to win a four-day week for you and your colleagues.

The best place to start is writing down all the key people at your organisation who are going to need persuading, whether it's the CEO, head of HR or just an influential and popular member of the team. Next, pull together a document that both makes the case and highlights the existing supportive evidence already out there.

Making the Case

The strongest argument is that moving to a four-day week is a 'win–win for workers and employers.' For workers: a better work–life balance allows people to live happier and more fulfilled lives, by providing more time for rest, leisure and 'life admin.' And, more importantly in this case, for employers: as we know, many workers are overworked, stressed and burnt out; whereas rested workers are better workers. A four-day week increases productivity, inspires creativity and helps employers recruit and retain high-quality staff.

You could use some of the arguments set out in Chapter One to make a more detailed case and the 4 Day Week Campaign website has a page highlighting lots of the benefits.[1]

Identify Successful Examples

Many businesses and organisations around the world have already successfully moved to a four-day week of around 32 hours, with no loss of pay for workers. Look for a workplace similar to yours in the full list of UK four-day-week employers in the resources section of this book. Get in touch with them if you think having an initial conversation might help your fact-gathering exercise. The case studies dotted throughout this book should also be useful.

Remember, there is no one-size-fits-all approach to a four-day week so recognise that implementation needs to suit your workplace's specific situation. This should be factored in when making the case to your boss.

---

[1] 4dayweek.co.uk/why

Persuading Your Colleagues

Speak with your colleagues to get an idea of their thoughts and feelings and see if you can persuade them. Alongside this, you could start a petition for them to sign. This effort will be strengthened with the support of your trade union representatives (if you have them) who can help you present the most effective case and represent you in negotiations. Additionally, a survey of all staff will give a clear indication of the breadth of support across the organisation, and provide an opportunity to address any concerns and fears, before presenting the case to your boss.

Persuade Your Bosses to Launch a Trial

Speak with your bosses (start with line managers and influential colleagues you have identified), show them successful examples and present the petition from your colleagues. Start by seeking a conversation about the benefits of the four-day week, rather than demanding it directly. Many bosses want to think it over and examine the issue before committing. A letter or email to your employer is a good way of pointing them in the right direction and the 4 Day Week Campaign website has a template letter you can use or adapt.[2] Feed your bosses our business benefits guide on a four-day week.[3]

Suggest launching a trial, or consider rolling it out department by department. An incremental approach can

---

[2] https://tinyurl.com/templatelettertoemployer

[3] https://tinyurl.com/4dayweekbusinessbenefitsguide

help iron out any operational obstacles, take away some of the fear and determine the best way for your organisation to reduce hours. Many bosses have already implemented the four-day week but there are good reasons why others will be sceptical and hesitant. Making your case in the most compelling way possible, and showing you have considered the challenges in advance, will really help.

If your workplace isn't unionised already, then look into trade union representation. This will give you more power and could make all the difference.

DEMAND A 4 DAY WEEK IN YOUR WORKPLACE -TOOLKIT

1. MAKING THE CASE

It's a win-win for workers and employers:

- Workers: A better work-life balance allows us to live happier and more fulfilled lives, by providing more time for rest, leisure and 'life admin'.
- Employers: Many workers are overworked, stressed and burnt out, whereas rested workers are better workers. A four-day week increases productivity, creativity and helps employers recruit and retain high-quality staff.

The 9 to 5, five-day working week is outdated and no longer fit for purpose.

- Covid has given us a one-off opportunity for a total rethink of the world of work.

See more benefits for workers, employers, the economy, society and environment: *4dayweek.co.uk/why*

2. IDENTIFY SUCCESSFUL EXAMPLES

Many businesses and organisations around the world have successfully reduced their working hours to a four-day week of around 32 hours, with no loss of pay for workers.

See the list of UK 4 Day Week Employers and identify a workplace similar to yours: *4dayweek.co.uk/employers*

There is no one-size-fits-all approach to a four-day week. Recognise that how your workplace implements a four-day week needs to suit your specific situation.

3. PERSUADE YOUR COLLEAGUES

Speak with your colleagues about it - get an idea of their thoughts and feelings and see if you can persuade them. This could be done via a work WhatsApp group.

Start a petition for your colleagues to sign, to later present to your bosses.

Engage your union representatives (if you have them) to help fight for reduced time.

4. PERSUADE YOUR BOSSES TO LAUNCH A TRIAL

Speak with your bosses (start with line managers) about the reasons and the successful examples, and present the petition from your colleagues.

Start by asking a conversation about the issue, rather than demanding it directly. Many bosses want to think it over and examine the issue before committing.

- Feed your bosses the latest research on a four-day week at *4dayweek.co.uk/research*

Suggest launching a trial first. Or consider rolling it out department-by-department.

- An incremental approach helps to iron out any operational obstacles and determine the best way for your organisation to reduce hours.

See our separate guide for employers: *4dayweek.co.uk/advice-for-employers*

9. The Future

"Since the 1980s the link between increasing productivity and expanding free time has been broken. It's time to put that right. We should work to live, not live to work."

John McDonnell MP, former Labour Party Shadow Chancellor (2015–2020)

I'm convinced a four-day week for all is going to be the future of work and I hope by this point you are at least more intrigued, if not yet entirely convinced. One day we are going to look back and marvel that we used to work five days a week, just as people look back now and scarcely believe the weekend needed to be invented. The movement has certainly come a long way in a short space of time but there is still a very long way to go. It's worth remembering it took the best part of two decades for the shift from a six-day week to a five-day week to ripple out across the economy so we know it will take time, even if it is long overdue.

A survey by the charity Be The Business found, in 2021, that 18 per cent of UK companies were considering moving to a four-day week and five per cent of small and medium-sized businesses already had. This means over one million UK firms and three million employees could move to a four-day week in the near future and nearly 300,000 small and medium-sized UK businesses with over 840,000 employees are already working a four-day week.

Our campaign has already had over 150 UK employer accreditations, which admittedly is a relatively small number, but things are heading in the right direction. As the most relevant comparison, when the Living Wage Foundation started out, only a handful of companies signed up. Today, it has over 13,000 accredited employers[1] and we want to achieve something similar. Some sectors are racing ahead, like marketing, gaming, tech and charity. So if you are a businessman or woman reading this, it's worth bearing in mind this warning from entrepreneur Andrew Barnes: *"Your biggest risk is not doing this. Your biggest risk is that your biggest competitor does it first."*

It's been pleasing to see policymakers in America and the UK taking note of the recent growing popularity by bringing forward some of the first legislation to create a national four-day week policy. Labour Party MP, and former Shadow Chief Secretary to the Treasury, Peter Dowd introduced a bill in the House of Commons in October 2022 to reduce the maximum working week to 32 hours, which would have effectively given every British worker the chance of moving to a four-day week.

The 32 Hour Working Week Bill was the first UK Parliamentary bill attempting to bring in a four-day working week. The bill sought to amend the Working Time

---

[1]. https://www.livingwage.org.uk/accredit

Regulations Act 1998 to reduce the maximum working week from 48 hours to 32. We inherited this legislation from the EU so it is going to need a post-Brexit update anyway. To ensure low-paid and underemployed workers have their incomes protected, the bill included a clause which would ensure an overtime rate of 1.5 times the worker's ordinary rate of pay for any time spent working beyond 32 hours per week.

Unfortunately progress of the bill has stalled but, speaking in the House of Commons, Labour MP Peter Dowd said:[2]

" It was almost exactly a century ago that British workers switched from working a six-day week to a five-day week. The pandemic has undoubtedly shaken up the world of work. We have already seen a huge rise in remote working, flexible working, part-time work, and yes, four-day working weeks. Change is coming, and the Government and my own party should grasp it. We could be leading the world in moving to a four-day week, and my Bill would enable us to do just that."

The bill was inspired by a similar piece of legislation that has now been proposed twice in the US House of Representatives by Democrat politician Mark Takano and has the support of the Congressional Progressive Caucus, a 100-strong group of members of Congress, founded by Bernie Sanders (among others) which includes the likes of Alexandria Ocasio-Cortez. This all builds upon

---

[2] https://hansard.parliament.uk/commons/2022-10-18/debates/8EAA165C-681F-4C1E-B697-B8B36F38AA50/WorkingTimeRegulations(Amendment) I will need to update the quote too as I've realised most of that quote was from a press release and not spoken in the House of Commons

the UK Labour Party's commitment at the 2019 General Election to bring in a four-day week within a decade, a policy spearheaded by the then Shadow Chancellor, John McDonnell MP, which made the party's manifesto.

To make the four-day week a reality in the UK, the 4 Day Week Campaign has released a Mini-Manifesto which we are asking all political parties to adopt ahead of the next General Election. The policies included would enable the transition to a four-day week with no loss of pay across the economy:

- A reduction to the maximum working week from 48 to 32 hours by 2030
- An amendment to official flexible working guidance to include the right for workers to request a four-day, 32-hour working week with no loss of pay
- A £100 million fund to support companies moving to a four-day, 32-hour working week
- A fully funded four-day week pilot in the public sector
- The establishment of a Working Time Council bringing together trade unions, industry leaders and business leaders to coordinate on policy for implementation of a shorter working week

But, at the end of the day, the four-day week is ultimately a choice about what kind of society we want to live in. It is a choice about whether to prioritise work or life. Do we want to continue on the path of busyness and distraction, with little sense of community? Or can we step back, slow down, and give ourselves the space to focus more on the joy and companionship we all seek in life? Of course, joy can arise at work, but it's usually in love, family, friendship, community and nature that we find true joy. If we can do all of this, while not sacrificing our work's productivity, then what have we got to lose?

Our culture today – especially in the UK, where our addiction to work takes precedence over everything else – needs to change. Overly valuing work and seeing being busy as a badge of honour is surely a sign of an unhealthy culture. As campaigners we're determined to finally get the work–life balance conundrum right so that on a very basic level, there is enough time outside work to properly enjoy life. What the four-day week is ultimately about is giving everyone the time to live happier and more fulfilled lives. We want to work to live, not live to work. I strongly believe that under a 9-5, five-day week model we simply don't have enough time to truly experience all the joys life has to offer. It sets us up to fail, with inadequate time to get everything done: cleaning, washing, childcare, paying bills, cooking, hobbies, relationships, friendships, visiting family. I could go on.

It's almost exactly a century since British workers switched from working a six-day to a five-day week. Yet the same old arguments made against the introduction of the weekend, against holiday pay, maternity pay, and the living wage are being wheeled out again today against a four-day working week. They say the economy will suffer. They were wrong then and they are wrong now, and the growing number of businesses adopting a four-day week successfully are proving them wrong.

Who will be the Ford Motor Company of the 21st Century? This is a question I'm sure will be answered in the coming years. Because it seems wherever the four-day week with no loss of pay has been trialled across the world, it's been a win-win for both workers and employers. Both productivity and workers' well-being has improved. All the evidence shows a four-day week would be good for workers, good for the economy and good for the environment. What have we got to lose by at least giving it a go?

The four-day week is surely the future of work and it's in our power to start making it happen. We don't have to sit around waiting for the Government. If this book has done anything, I hope it's shown you that, and offered practical support to guide you on your journey to a four-day week. Over to you now for implementation!

Acknowledgements

I would like to say a huge thank you to my colleague Joe Moore, Business Network Coordinator at the 4 Day Week Campaign, for writing the brilliant chapter on improving business performance.

I would also like to thank my tremendously talented colleague Kyle Lewis, Co-Director at the think tank Autonomy, for his help with chapter three and words of advice.

Finally, I would like to thank my editor Martin Hickman, who reached out to me with the opportunity at the perfect moment. His edits, advice and feedback have been invaluable.

Resources

- Find out when the next 4 Day Week Rollout Programme is being run – a programme offered by the 4 Day Week Campaign and Autonomy to support organisations with moving to a four-day week: https://www.4dayweek.co.uk/rollout-programme
- The 4 Day Week Campaign website has a number of helpful resources: https://www.4dayweek.co.uk/resources
- To become an accredited four-day week employer, see: https://www.4dayweek.co.uk/employers
- The full results of the UK four-day week pilot can be read here: https://autonomy.work/portfolio/uk4dwpilotresults/
- Autonomy is a British think tank with a focus on the future of work and shorter working weeks. They also run a shorter working week consultancy service: https://autonomy.work/consultancy-2/

Academics and Researchers Who May Be Able to Help or Advise on Measuring the Success of a Trial:

- Juliet Schor (Professor of Sociology at Boston College)
- Brendan Burchell (Professor in the Social Sciences at the University of Cambridge)
- Dr David Frayne (Sociologist of Work at University of Salford)
- 4 Day Week Global is a not-for-profit community established by Andrew Barnes and Charlotte Lockhart: https://www.4dayweek.com/
- Entrepreneur and CEO Banks Benitez offers a range of consultancy services: https://www.banksbenitez.com/
- The Work Time Reduction Center of Excellence offer a range of services and is worth checking out: https://worktimereduction.com/
- A full list of 4 Day Week Campaign UK Accredited Organisations:

Name	Date started 4DW	Industry
3D Issue	2020	Digital
448 Studio	2022	Media
5 Squirrels Ltd	2022	Manufacturing
64 Million Artists	2020	Creative Industries
92 Minutes Ltd	2022	Consultancy
Accurise	2022	Accountancy
Acuity Solutions	2021	Consultancy

Name	Date started 4DW	Industry
Advantage Business Partnerships	2017	Professional Services
Advice Direct Scotland	2018	Charity
Agricultural Recruitment Specialists	2023	Recruitment
Amity Community Action	2021	NGO
Ascendancy	2023	Digital
Atlas Translations	2019	Travel
Atom Bank	2021	Banking
Autonomy	2022	NGO
Awin	2021	Marketing
Barefoot Architects	2020	Architect
Barking and Dagenham Giving	2023	Charity
BiBO	2018	Architect
Big Potato Games	2019	Gaming
BJP Consulting Group Ltd	2022	Consulting
Blink	2018	Marketing
Brett Nicholls Associates	2019	Accountancy
Butcher Bayley Architects	2020	Architect
Camlas	2023	Public Affairs
Causeway Irish Housing Association	2019	Housing
Charlton Morris	2021	Recruitment
Centre for Local Economic Strategies	2023	NGO
City to Sea	2022	NGO
CIVO	2022	Digital

Name	Date started 4DW	Industry
CMD: Studio	2021	Gaming
CMG Technologies	2015	Manufacturing
Coltech Global	2022	Technology
Common Knowledge	2021	Digital
Cooked Illustrations	2021	Media
Counting King Limited	2022	Consultancy
Crystallised	2019	Marketing
DataLase	2022	Technology
DigiLab	2022	Marketing
Digital Guerilla Consultancy	2017	Construction
Earth Science Partnership	2020	Engineering
Elektra Lighting	2019	Design
Element Four	2022	Consultancy
Escape the City	2021	Recruitment
ESG Gaming	2022	Gaming
Esteem Training	2020	Construction
Evolved Search	2021	Marketing
Flocc	2018	Marketing
FMC Global Talent	2021	Recruitment
Formedix	2019	Technology
Fortem People LTD	2022	Recruitment
Forward Space	2021	Design
Four Day Week Ltd	2019	Recruitment
Future Economy Scotland	2023	NGO
Geeks for Social Change	2021	IT
Giant Digital	2022	Consultancy
Girling Jones	2022	Recruitment

Name	Date started 4DW	Industry
Global Partners Digital	2022	Digital
Good Ancestor Movment	2021	Finance
Gracefruit	2020	Retail
Greenpost	2022	Recruitment
Gungho Marketing	2022	Marketing
Happy	2022	Learning
HearFocus	2021	Healthcare
Hello Heat Pumps	2022	Housing
Hello Starling	2018	Advertising
Highfield Professional Solutions	2021	Engineering
Hutch Games Ltd	2022	Gaming
Infigo	2022	IT/ Software
Intercultural Youth Scotland	2023	NGO
JMK Solicitors	2020	Legal
Legacy Events	2021	Events
Lemongrass Marketing	2022	Marketing
LIT Communication	2022	Marketing
Literal Humans	2022	Marketing
LUX - The Food & Drink Agency	2020	Advertising
MATS Consultancy	2021	Professional Services
Middle Child Theatre	2023	Creative Industries
Muckle Media	2023	Public Affairs
MRL Consulting	2019	Recruitment
Neohive	2022	Gaming
NEON (New Economy Organisers Network)	2021	NGO
New Vision Digital Marketing	2022	Digital
Opportunity Green	2023	Charity

Name	Date started 4DW	Industry
Oriel Square	2017	Education
Original Consultants	2021	Technology
Ormiston Wire Ltd	2020	Manufacturing
Paul David Smith Photography	2020	Creative Industries
Pollard Media	2021	Marketing
Pool Data	2022	Technology
Portcullis Legals	2019	Legal
Principles Agency	2022	Marketing
PTHR	2019	Design
Punch Creative	2020	Marketing
PureFluent	2019	Marketing
Quality of Life Foundation	2021	Charity
Reboot	2021	Marketing
Resilience Brokers	2021	NGO
Reward Agency	2020	Marketing
Richard John Andrews Ltd	2022	Architect
Roach Matthews Architects	2022	Architect
SDX Messaging	2022	Consultancy
Sensat	2023	Construction
SEOMG!	2020	Technology
Sidequest Ltd	2022	Gaming
Sinister Fish Games	2022	Gaming
Social Enterprise Direct	2020	Professional Services
Social For Good	2023	Marketing
Softer Success	2022	Consultancy
Sounds Like These	2022	Creative Industries
STC Expeditions	2020	Travel

Name	Date started 4DW	Industry
STOP AIDS	2019	Charity
streamGO	2021	Events
Synergy Vision	2018	Marketing
T-Cup	2021	Consultancy
Tailored Thinking	2022	HR
Talewind	2021	Gaming
Target Composites Ltd	2022	Manufacturing
Target Publishing	2021	Media
TBL Services	2022	Consultancy
Team Custard Kraken	2019	Gaming
Team Norse Thunder	2022	Sport
Technovent	2021	Manufacturing
The Circle	2020	Charity
Think Productive	2011	Consultancy
This Is Beyond	2021	Events
THRYVE	2021	Recruitment
Time Appointments	2022	Recruitment
Tribera	2022	Digital
Trigger	2023	Creative Industries
Trio Media	2022	Marketing
Tyler Grange Group Ltd	2022	Consultancy
Uniqodo	2022	Technology
UPAC Group	2021	Manufacturing
Vault City Brewing	2022	Manufacturing
Venture Stream	2021	Marketing
Vetro Recruitment	2023	Recruitment
We Are Purposeful	2022	NGO
Wellbeing Economy Alliance	2023	NGO

Name	Date started 4DW	Industry
Whering	2023	Digital
Whyfield	2022	Accountancy
Woven Ink Studio Limited	2018	Creative Industries
Xaso	2020	Marketing
You HR Consultancy	2023	Consultancy
YWCA Scotland	2021	Charity
Zync Digital	2018	Marketing

Index

Joe Ryle

Joe Ryle is Director of Britain's 4 Day Week Campaign. He is Media and Comms Lead for the think tank Autonomy, a former adviser to Shadow Chancellor John McDonnell MP and a former Labour Party Press Officer.

More titles from Canbury Press

Citizens
Why the Key to Fixing Everything is All of Us
Jon Alexander

MCKINSEY TOP 5 RECOMMENDED READ

'An underground hit'
Best Politics Books, Financial Times

More titles from Canbury Press

TikTok Boom
The Inside Story of the World's Favourite App
Chris Stokel-Walker

'It is rare for a business analysis to read like a thriller – this one does.'
Azeem Azhar, Founder, Exponential View